IN THE COMPUTER AGE
General Editor: André Jute

PUBLICATIONS
or professional communicators

André Jute

Batsford

Contents

In all the preceding roughs only the overall appearance of the publications was approved, specifically in terms of the audience expectation. I deliberately showed nothing detailed enough to delay us with specific discussion of graphical matters; I claimed to have no idea of which font I would recommend, though in fact the choice had already been narrowed down to four, including the font already in use.

Logically, the designer should progress from the approved overall appearance of the publication to the detailed work of grid, font selection and style definition, and the multiple other tasks of a new layout. But the real world does not work like that. In advance the client often wants to see what the display headline looks like or requires a rough label on a can for the sales director to try out on lead customers. In magazines the financial realities of distribution and advertising are such that the flag and the cover, which ideally should flow structurally from the interior, are always required immediately for pre-selling.

Resist the temptation to show illustration or headline positions on the grid at this stage of its development. To integrate illustrations and headlines properly with the grid, the text face must first be chosen, together with its interline spacing or leading. But the text face is always chosen in association with the display face to be used for setting headlines and other large matter. As you can see, the process of publication design is not neatly compartmentalized.

The choice of typefaces is the most important function performed by the graphic designer. There is a school of thought which makes an arguable case that a graphic designer is merely a typographer with some additional tacked-on minor skills. Until halfway through the twentieth century graphic designers were always called typographers. Even designers destined to spend their careers in television start their training with typography because their instructors believe that the letterform is the mother of all styled communication.

Contents

8

We shall make no routine distinction between theory and practice. Instead we shall deal with practical worked examples, breaking for theory only where absolutely unavoidable. Designers on a job have little time for theory, and in any event learn best the hard way, from experience.

Few things are more tiresome than a designer dissecting someone else's design and reaching only wrong conclusions because the constraints are unknown. Therefore all the examples in this book are chosen because I have intimate knowledge of the reasoning behind each decision. We shall work thoroughly through only a few relevant examples, so that all aspects of a complete job will be illuminated.

The most challenging of our examples is the simple hobbyist magazine, because it placed the largest number of conflicting demands on the designer. The high level, full colour publications illustrated are easier work for an experienced designer simply because there are fewer constraints.

The control grid is, next to movable type itself, the most useful invention in the history of graphic design.

The control grid is a graphic designer's multiplication tool. It makes every hour of the most humble DTP operator count for four, and every hour of a top designer is worth a thousand by courtesy of the grid. It helps a designer place copy precisely even on hungover mornings. It also offers the same designer immortality.

The great advantage of the grid is repeatability. Once the grid is set by the designer, huge magazines or books can be created in that image by assistants. Should the designer leave for greener pastures, the design lives on in the hands of the publisher who paid for it. The grid enables even a modestly financed publisher to call in a top designer to design a magazine, which will be made up by less exhorbitantly rewarded operators.

The graphic design control grid is the great unsung hero of our culture. Create it with care. Honour and observe it.

No typographer's education is ever completed. The best designers are those who learn something new about their craft every day. And the bedrock of their craft is the letterform.

This book is about the whole publication, so we have merely touched on the art of typography. The great designers are distinguished by knowing much more of the minutiae of the letterform and its application, indeed by being obsessive about it. A good place to extend or refresh your knowledge is *Typography* by Grant Shipcott, also in this series. You already know Grant: he is the production manager and typesetter on the two magazines we are using as extended examples.

We now turn to the layout of the publication. 'Layout' is designer's shorthand for how the typography is arranged and, more, how it meshes with the other graphic elements found in any publication: lines, pictures whether illustrations or photographs, and of course colour when it is available.

Thanksgiving

All illustrations are by André Jute exclusively in Aldus, Claris and Letraset Studio software, except:

pp14-16 in MacDraw Pro © Claris International

p17 page design by Colleen Burnham and architectural rendering by Stuart Silk in Aldus FreeHand © Aldus Corporation

p31 in Letraset ColorStudio © Esselte Letraset

p64 by Charles Jute in Aldus SuperPaint © Charles Jute

pp75-5 in MacDraw Pro © Claris International

p87 by Phillip G Gordon in Aldus SuperPaint © Aldus Corporation

pp92-3 illustration by André Jute based on a photograph © Rosalind Pain-Hayman

pp22-23, p81 and p87, cover designs by André Jute with

illustration p22, right, and p87 in Aldus Freehand © Vicky Squires

and illustration p23, right, and p81in Adobe Illustrator by Jill Skinner and Hugh Skinner © Hugh Skinner

p66 and pp83-3 from *Videographics* © Hugh Skinner

pp88-9 from *Illustration* © Vicky Squires

all published in the series

Graphic Design in the Computer Age

by B. T. Batsford Ltd, London

Art in examples the work of André Jute but the copyright of Writers News Ltd by permission

Photograph p6 © Rosalind Pain-Hayman

Her photograph by courtesy of Jilly Cooper

Author's photograph by Paddy Boyle, used by courtesy of Writers News Ltd

Some of these graphics are repeated on the part titles and the contents pages

Jacket and interior design by André Jute

Typeset and originated by Create Colour Bureau, Bath

Printed in Singapore for the publisher

B. T. Batsford Ltd

4 Fitzhardinge Street, London W1H 0AH

1

Publications

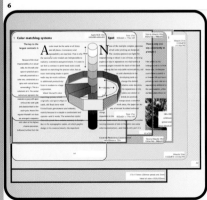

Almost everywhere in the world a publication is defined by the law on libel as whatever is made known to one or more persons by the medium of print or broadcast. That includes anything from a postcard sent to a friend through newsletters and newspapers to television and radio. A graphic designer is a mass communicator, which excludes the letter to an individual. A graphic designer is a visual communicator, which excludes radio. *Every other mass communication* is the graphic designer's meat.

This book covers the most of important of these mass communications, printed publications. Other books in this series cover each of the other main media, and these are supported by books detailing basic underlying principles or skills, such as illustration, colour selection, and type choice. Here we shall touch on the other media as required by the interdependence of the multimedia society we live in, and highlight the other skills and basic disciplines as they are applied to the making of printed publications.

Let no one persuade you that making quality publications is easy or quick, but resist the mystifiers who claim that success is impossible unless you possess multiple arcane skills. Keep your head and proceed methodically. With practice you will, much more quickly than you imagined possible, acquire skill and confidence to handle the technical requirements with minimum effort—leaving you free to apply your conscious energy to creativity.

Good luck!

Everything printed to inform, entertain & persuade

A publication of which only twelve copies were made, to enable a decision to be taken on which monitor screens to buy. It shows various likely documents at full size and reduced on the commercially available screen sizes, with the usable screen area indicated. The decision reached, to buy the largest available screens, was that desired by the designer of this publication. Persuasion defines a successful publication.

1 Color matching systems

Spot

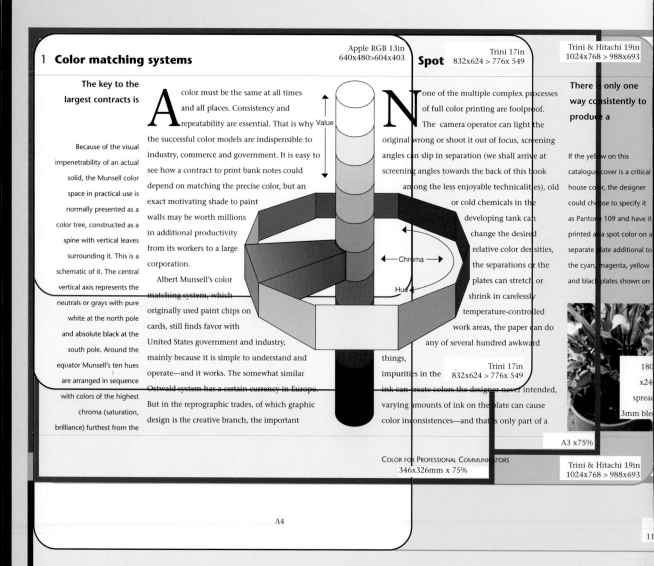

Apple RGB 13in
640x480>604x403

Trini 17in
832x624 > 776x 549

Trini & Hitachi 19in
1024x768 > 988x693

The key to the largest contracts is

A color must be the same at all times and all places. Consistency and repeatability are essential. That is why the successful color models are indispensible to industry, commerce and government. It is easy to see how a contract to print bank notes could depend on matching the precise color, but an exact motivating shade to paint walls may be worth millions in additional productivity from its workers to a large corporation.

Albert Munsell's color matching system, which originally used paint chips on cards, still finds favor with United States government and industry, mainly because it is simple to understand and operate—and it works. The somewhat similar Ostwald system has a certain currency in Europe. But in the reprographic trades, of which graphic design is the creative branch, the important

Because of the visual impenetrability of an actual solid, the Munsell color space in practical use is normally presented as a color tree, constructed as a spine with vertical leaves surrounding it. This is a schematic of it. The central vertical axis represents the neutrals or grays with pure white at the north pole and absolute black at the south pole. Around the equator Munsell's ten hues are arranged in sequence with colors of the highest chroma (saturation, brilliance) furthest from the

Value

Chroma

Hue

None of the multiple complex processes of full color printing are foolproof. The camera operator can light the original wrong or shoot it out of focus, screening angles can slip in separation (we shall arrive at screening angles towards the back of this book among the less enjoyable technicalities), old or cold chemicals in the developing tank can change the desired relative color densities, the separations or the plates can stretch or shrink in carelessly temperature-controlled work areas, the paper can do any of several hundred awkward things, impurities in the ink can create colors the designer never intended, varying amounts of ink on the plate can cause color inconsistences—and that is only part of a

Trini 17in
832x624 > 776x 549

There is only one way consistently to produce a

If the yellow on this catalogue cover is a critical house color, the designer could choose to specify it as Pantone 109 and have it printed as a spot color on a separate plate additional to the cyan, magenta, yellow and black plates shown on

180
x24
spread
3mm ble

A3 x75%

Trini & Hitachi 19in
1024x768 > 988x693

COLOR FOR PROFESSIONAL COMMUNICATORS
346x326mm x 75%

A4

11

173+173mm x326mm spread and 3mm
bleed all sides =352x332mm

Hitachi 21in
1152x870
>1116x795

0
n
d
l

Hitachi 21in
:870 >1116x795

A3

Almost everywhere in the world a publication is defined by the law on libel as whatever is made known to one or more persons by the medium of print or broadcast. That includes anything from a postcard sent to a friend through newsletters and newspapers to television and radio. A graphic designer is a mass communicator, which excludes the letter to an individual. A graphic designer is a visual communicator, which excludes radio. *Every other mass communication* is the graphic designer's meat.

This book covers the most of important of these mass communications, printed publications. Other books in this series cover each of the other main media, and these are supported by books detailing basic underlying principles or skills, such as illustration, colour selection, and type choice. Here we shall touch on the other media as required by the interdependence of the multimedia society we live in, and highlight the other skills and basic disciplines as they are applied to the making of printed publications.

Let no one persuade you that making quality publications is easy or quick, but resist the mystifiers who claim that success is impossible unless you possess multiple arcane skills. Keep your head and proceed methodically. With practice you will, much more quickly than you imagined possible, acquire skill and confidence to handle the technical requirements with minimum effort—leaving you free to apply your conscious energy to creativity.

Good luck!

Everything printed to inform, entertain & persuade

A publication of which only twelve copies were made, to enable a decision to be taken on which monitor screens to buy. It shows various likely documents at full size and reduced on the commercially available screen sizes, with the usable screen area indicated. The decision reached, to buy the largest avialable screens, was that desired by the designer of this publication. Persuasion defines a successful publication.

Examples

We shall make no routine distinction between theory and practice. Instead we shall deal with practical worked examples, breaking for theory only where absolutely unavoidable. Designers on a job have little time for theory, and in any event learn best the hard way, from experience.

Few things are more tiresome than a designer dissecting someone else's design and reaching only wrong conclusions because the constraints are unknown. Therefore all the examples in this book are chosen because I have intimate knowledge of the reasoning behind each decision. We shall work thoroughly through only a few relevant examples, so that all aspects of a complete job will be illuminated.

The most challenging of our examples is the simple hobbyist magazine, because it placed the largest number of conflicting demands on the designer. The high level, full colour publications illustrated are easier work for an experienced designer simply because there are fewer constraints.

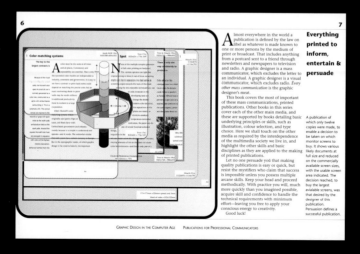

2

client & brief

The client: important people at Writers News Ltd

David St John Thomas, publisher Thirty years of experience publishing hobbyist books. Also a leading mail order operator. His dream since childhood had been his own magazine but his only experience was very recent, with a small subscription magazine. He did however know his market (writers) intimately, being a writer 'one of them', and having owned a correspondence school for writers. Firm ideas on the purpose and function of design, and the downside of design for its own sake. Decidedly unenthusiastic about white space.

Richard Bell, editor By far the most experienced editor of writers' magazines in Europe. He had edited the main competition, then run David's correspondence college and founded and edited David's subscription magazine. Convinced, as is his publisher, that a reader not interested in the main article on any page should be offered an alternative. Therefore keen on short continuations and 'fillers'—even to the extent of creating space for them where they do not exist!

There is rarely only a single client

Carol Pope, news editor In control of the content and makeup of her own twelve pages of news. A convert to DTP and the proud owner of a Mac, she takes pride in delivering copy that fits to the word. Like every other hard news journalist, who all deal in a product with a currency of days, at most weeks, she had a hard time accepting that proper design fixes rules for good and then makes arrangements for enforcing those rules. Impressed with the capabilities of the new technology, she wanted pictures at angles and "curliques". Her major problem was squeezing in more words.

Grant Shipcott, in charge of production A typographer by training, he would be responsible for maintaining the integrity of the design once the consultant designer had finished the job and left. Grant is not an employee of Writers News Ltd but runs XL Publishing Services, offering typesetting and other services to publishers. While the magazine was being designed the designer worked out of Grant's offices.

André Jute, designer

The client: important people at Writers News Ltd

David St John Thomas, publisher Thirty years of experience publishing hobbyist books. Also a leading mail order operator. His dream since childhood had been his own magazine but his only experience was very recent, with a small subscription magazine. He did however know his market (writers) intimately, being as a writer 'one of them', and having owned a correspondence school for writers. Firm ideas on the purpose and function of design, and the downside of design for its own sake. Decidedly unenthusiastic about white space.

Richard Bell, editor By far the most experienced editor of writers' magazines in Europe. He had edited the main competition, then run David's correspondence college and founded and edited David's subscription magazine. Convinced, as is his publisher, that a reader not interested in the main article on any page should be offered an alternative. Therefore keen on short continuations and 'fillers'—even to the extent of creating space for them where they do not exist!

There is rarely only a single client

Carol Pope, news editor In control of the content and makeup of her own twelve pages of news. A convert to DTP and the proud owner of a Mac, she takes pride in delivering copy that fits to the word. Like every other hard news journalist, who all deal in a product with a currency of days, at most weeks, she had a hard time accepting that proper design fixes rules for good and then makes arrangements for enforcing those rules. Impressed with the capabilities of the new technology, she wanted pictures at angles and 'curliques'. Her major problem was squeezing in more words.

Grant Shipcott, in charge of production A typographer by training, he would be responsible for maintaining the integrity of the design once the consultant designer had finished the job and left. Grant is not an employee of Writers News Ltd but runs XL Publishing Services, offering typesetting and other services to publishers. While the magazine was being designed the designer worked out of Grant's offices.

André Jute, designer

Successful use of graphic design in any periodical depends on continuing firm control

This is what happens to a perfectly good design when no one is in charge of its maintenance and the typesetter and printer do as they please. Elements not lining up, a liquorice all-sorts of type. It was no-one's fault because no one was responsible for control until Grant arrived.

Where is the client coming from?

The client, David Thomas, first brought in Grant Shipcott as a production consultant. By the time Grant had brought execution of the magazine back into line with the original concept, the design had become obsolete.

The original design, left, consisted of the news pages wrapped around the sort of features one can find in most hobbyist magazines. In the beginning David and editor Richard Bell did not know how many words they could afford or even obtain, so the magazine had to look thick enough to be worth the money but not use too many words. That was the purpose of those blue bars, to use up space. By now, with the magazine having a substantial subscription sale, they had discovered that they could get more news and features than they could ever use, and at reasonable cost. In fact the magazine was straining at the seams.

David in the meantime had conceived a far greater ambition, selling a magazine for writers on the newsstand. Originally I was brought in to design the newsstand magazine, with a light redesign of the news pages thrown in as a sort of makeshift to make it worth the expense. As it turned out, much more time was spent on the news pages than on the features, partly because of the presuppositions that came with the news pages but not with the features sections.

Newspapers and news pages in magazines are design challenges because they are so bitty. By contrast advertisements and feature pages are easier because they are usually built around a single theme.

Pantone Matching System number 300, the blue of the *Writers News* flag. Was it by now so strongly associated with the magazine that publisher and designer would consider it too high a risk to change?

David St John Thomas explains how an aware client chooses a designer—

"A publisher with several hundred book jackets to design every year—thousands over a career—of course comes to know many designers. They fall into three classes: those who do what the client tells them to do, those who make pretty pictures, and the top designers who are the entrepreneurs of communication.

'In books a mistake is expensive but can be rectified by rejacketing. A magazine is an investment of a greater magnitude altogether. A magazine destined for the newsstand gets only one chance. If it doesn't succeed immediately, your distributors fade into the night even before your advertisers desert you. It is not a question of whether the return from the magazine will in the short term justify the cost of a top designer but whether, without the right designer, there will be a magazine at all. A magazine requires deep pockets.

'I already knew the ideal designer for this job because I published some of his books.

'Besides being formidably experienced as a designer, André Jute had several other kinds of experience relevant to precisely my problems. He had been on the executive side in a large advertising agency and later managing editor of a magazine group, so I didn't have to explain advertising, managerial and financial considerations to him twice. As he had a dozen published novels I could count on him to understand the aspirations of my target market. Best of all, he had even written a successful book for other writers, *Writing a Thriller,* just then going into a third expanded edition.

'Survival proves I made the right choice."

—and his precise aims with his magazines

" Besides being a dream of mine, there was financial sense in launching the newsstand magazine. The cost of recruiting each subscriber to our existing subscription magazine was so high that we had to keep a subscriber three years before we broke even on the cost of recruitment.

'I also suspected that we did not reach a substantial part of our target market because none of the available advertising media covered them economically.

'My plan was therefore to launch the newsstand magazine as a quarterly to start with. It would consist of the much enlarged features and services sections from the existing monthly subscription magazine. But it would *not* have the substantial news section of the subscription magazine. Receiving the news of markets opening up for writers, opportunities to sell work, and competitions, would be the lure to persuade buyers of the newsstand magazine to subscribe. If enough did, the cost would fall.

'It was immediately obvious that for the newsstand quarterly the features section would have to be upgraded and redesigned—a long overdue exercise because we had outgrown the previous design—and that it would require at least a colour cover.

'To save production costs in the months when the newsstand quarterly appeared, subscribers would receive the news pages as a wraparound to the quarterly magazine.

'The newsstand magazine would have to sell enough copies and attract enough advertising to pay its own way.

'Good design helped my dream come true. "

The needs of the target audience determines the limits of graphic design

In our magazine example every decision-maker at the client and both the outside consultants (Grant and I) were published writers. Between us we could therefore speak with some authority on who the market for a magazine for writers would be and make well-educated guesses about their demands.

Be warned, this is a minority case. Even in hobbyist magazines this much market knowledge is rare. There are only two reasonably common cases of print publications sharing such a high level of market certainty. The obvious one is advertisements for the most sophisticated, largest and richest clients, who can afford a fine quality of market research. The other is a newsletter for a small, well-integrated, homogenous workforce—and this case is not as common as one might first believe. At Hilton hotels worldwide the managerial staff all speak English, the executive cooks have at least recipe French, but the rest of the staff speak over 160 languages.

Stuart Silk Architects is a Seattle-based firm specializing in historical renovations and custom residences, such as the design pictured here in this sectional drawing.

PROBLEM
The client wanted a small house with open, yet defined spaces. It was also important that the spatial qualities be felt from the upper two floors to make the house seem larger.

SOLUTION
A circulation spine organizes the plan on the upper two floors to allow for a configuration of adjacent spaces. A vaulted ceiling in the living room serves as the link to the second story.

AESTHETICS
The design fits into its neighborhood through its scale, sloping roof, and window and column designs. As a contemporary counterpoint, it uses striped stucco, abstracted eaves, a metal canopy at the entrance, and exposed steel columns.

MEGAHols

A designer who wants to do effective work must insist that the client defines the market as closely as possible. The purpose is to deduce what the readers will expect to gain from the advertisement, newsletter, newspaper, magazine, brochure, flyer or service manual.

These are the minimum 'market' questions the client must answer before the designer starts work:

What do potential users share?
    sex
    race
    income
    social standing or attitude ('lifestyle')
    peer group or profession
    common interest

How/when will they use the publication?
    gleefully (hobbyists)
    purposefully (professionals)
    casually (general magazine readers)
    hurriedly (newspaper readers)

How often will they see the publication? Over what period?

What is the outlook of the typical reader?
    conservative
    forward looking, avant-garde
    somewhere in between

Are there any sensitive issues that need to be avoided or given special attention?

Anything else you want to tell me? May I see your research please?

Graphic design integrates message, medium and market

The market for the holiday poster and for the architect's brochure may be the same people—but they would use the publications differently, glancing at the poster but studying the brochure. That is why the poster permits any dream to be read into the illustration, while the brochure has a very specific illustration and space for explanatory text.

Roughs to match message to market

In our example the typical user of the publication is someone who has retired young and taken up writing as a second occupation. Race and sex are irrelevant; most are comfortable rather than rich. They can be counted on to study the magazine carefully, so no startling tricks are required.

This audience is likely to be slightly more conservative than the general population, yet of open mind. But they are too sophisticated to put any premium at all on fine design if it comes at the cost of essential information.

It was imperative that the new layout offer the maximum number of words consonant with decent design and readability. David Thomas had brought from hobby book

It is unlikely that any real page would ever carry all the elements shown on some of these, but their availability had to be demonstrated.

publishing, where perceived value is an important sales tool, a dislike of 'wasted' white space. Such white space as could

be justified would therefore have to work hard for its living. Richard Bell wanted the opportunity to 'mess up the page somewhat' to give even the most hard-to-please reader something interesting on every page; some of the four column sketches overleaf were made to show how irreconcilable this demand is with good design. More positively, the designs above show the flexibility of a 'cleaner' concept.

Notice the grey blocks of one-sixth page advertisements, a pain to integrate, shown even at the rough visual stage. Editorial staff might not care but you may be certain the advertising executives will ask. Professionals don't wait to be told to do a necessary job.

No mistake about it, the blue was my least favourite element in the existing design. But already it was dawning on us that we were changing so many other things, changing the blue as well could be too much. In an ideal world a designer would change one element, test it, then change another. The cost would of course be horrendous—but the result would communicate perfectly.

Always show service and news pages in your roughs

News editor Carol Pope wanted more words in her finite twelve pages and it was a pleasure to give them to her in a brand new design as a combination of a larger print area, a narrower typeface, a smaller typesize, reduced leading, and more flexible headlines—all concepts we shall meet in making the detailed design. Even though I was willing to consider it, her desire for pictures at an angle—one is shown on page 18—mustered no support from her colleagues and the idea was dropped. As for 'curliques', script faces and

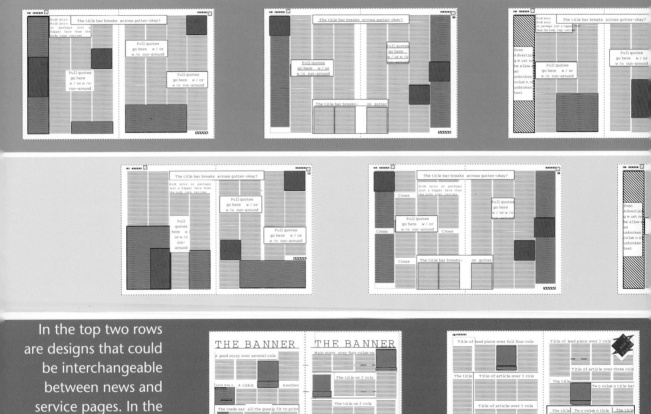

In the top two rows are designs that could be interchangeable between news and service pages. In the bottom row, news covers and exclusively news pages.

other pointless decorations, I wouldn't even discuss them, instead offering irregular runarounds of retouched photographs.

Except for the cover of the news magazine, which would have one spot colour, and the full colour cover of the newsstand quarterly, there would be no colour. The cost saving was substantial but the deciding reason was that colour photographs of the requisite quality would not be regularly available.

The tinted boxes shown were later dropped because of technical difficulties.

Agreement on overall appearance of news and service pages

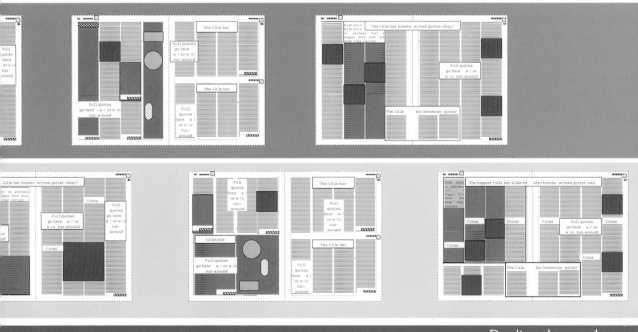

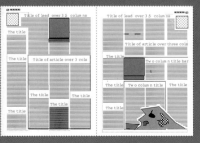

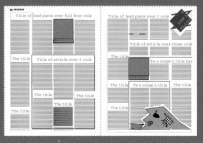

Don't make roughs too smooth. Clients dislike being steamrollered. These visuals were computer generated but then roughed-up for casual presentation.

The final arbiter is always the consumer

When I conceived the series this book belongs to—and this book too—I worked backwards from the final consumer, a designer just like you. The entire series arose from the unsuitability of most of the handbooks on the market for my purposes as a practising designer, but it would be a mistake to say I created the series for me, or for the publisher financing the books. Instead I identified five groups of people crucially interested in graphic design at various levels:

Graphic designers who recently left college and started work. I can easily remember how when I started I prayed for a book with some answers.

Trained graphic designers who want a quick refresher on something they haven't touched for years. We are in an expansive, specialized and fast-changing profession. No one can know everything.

The new breed of DTP designers. These are the designers created by the desktop computer who have no graphics training at

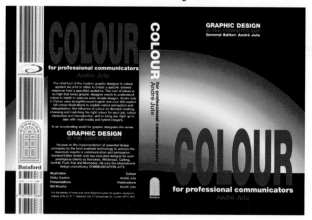

all. They are however often highly trained and skilled in other disciplines and used to teaching themselves new skills out of books.

Executives, not designers themselves, with graphic design supervision responsibility. These are the clients of designers and consist of executives in marketing and product management, publishing, public relations, politics, and a vast number of other industries which live or die by their communication with their target consumer.

Students still being trained as graphic designers. They would benefit most from books written to be useful to their professional peer group. In any event, I used to hate the plodding textbooks of my college days—soon proven irrelevant in practice—and believe students are a lot smarter than they are often given credit for.

If you belong to one of these groups, you are the client who paid for this series. You can judge for yourself how persuasively we communicate with you.

In this example *you* are the ultimate client

The inside of these books were intended 'to be a kaleidoscope of good design' but on the outside the various designers had to express their individuality within a strict grid designed to unite the series on the bookstore shelf. For more rigidly controlled examples, check your local supermarket.

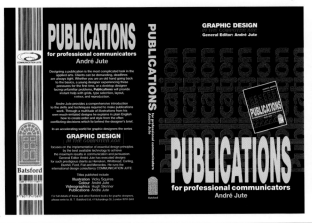

In all the preceding roughs only the overall appearance of the publications was approved, specifically in terms of the audience expectation. I deliberately showed nothing detailed enough to delay us with specific discussion of graphical matters; I claimed to have no idea of which font I would recommend, though in fact the choice had already been narrowed down to four, including the font already in use.

Logically, the designer should progress from the approved overall appearance of the publication to the detailed work of grid, font selection and style definition, and the multiple other tasks of a new layout. But the real world does not work like that. In ads the client often wants to see what the display headline looks like or requires a rough label on a can for the sales director to try out on lead customers. In magazines the financial realities of distribution and advertising are such that the flag and the cover, which ideally should flow structurally from the interior, are always required immediately for pre-selling.

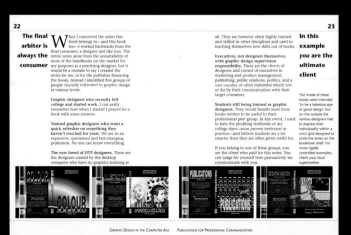

22

The final arbiter is always the consumer

When I conceived the series this book belongs to—and this book too—I worked backwards from the final consumer, a designer just like you. The entire series arose from the unsuitability of most of the handbooks on the market for my purposes as a practising designer, but it would be a mistake to say I created the series for me, or for the publisher financing the books. Instead I identified five groups of people crucially interested in graphic design at various levels:

Graphic designers who recently left college and started work. I can easily remember how when I started I prayed for a book with some answers.

Trained graphic designers who want a quick refresher on something they haven't touched for years. We are in an expansive, specialized and fast-changing profession. No one can know everything.

The new breed of DTP designers. These are the designers created by the desktop computer who have no graphics training at all. They are however often highly trained and skilled in other disciplines and used to teaching themselves new skills out of books.

Executives, not designers themselves, with graphic design supervision responsibility. These are the clients of designers and consist of executives in marketing and product management, publishing, public relations, politics, and a vast number of other industries which live or die by their communication with their target consumer.

Students still being trained as graphic designers. They would benefit most from books written to be useful to their professional peer group. In any event, I used to hate the plodding textbooks of my college days—soon proven irrelevant in practice—and believe students are a lot smarter than they are often given credit for.

If you belong to one of these groups, you are the client who paid for this series. You can judge for yourself how persuasively we communicate with you.

23

In this example *you* are the ultimate client

The inside of these books were intended 'to be a kaleidoscope of good design' but on the outside the various designers had to express their individuality within a strict grid designed to unite the series on the bookstore shelf. For more rigidly controlled examples, check your local supermarket.

GRAPHIC DESIGN IN THE COMPUTER AGE   PUBLICATIONS FOR PROFESSIONAL COMMUNICATORS

3

Flag & cover

The flag lies at the cutting edge of selling any magazine to its intended audience

The flag of the magazine or newspaper is that part of the cover which includes the nameplate, the date of issue, and often other information. It is wrong to call it the masthead, a name that should be reserved for the listing on the inside somewhere of all the editorial, legal and financial officers of the publisher.

The flag is extremely important because it carries the major burden of distinguishing the publication on the newsstand, where there will be many other publications vying for the customer's attention and money. Even a tied company newsletter has competition from everything else on the worker's desk, and should appeal for his attention accordingly.

Writing
MAGAZINE

Spring 1992   From the publishers of **WRITERS NEWS**

the subscription monthly was excluded from use in the newsstand quarterly. Instead we decided not to have a house colour at all, though the blue would stay with the subscription monthly for the foreseeable future, and would be used as a mnemonic link to the sister magazine on the cover of the newstand quarterly.

Instead of a house colour, which can be limiting, we would change the outline—the red above—to suit the balance of colour on the cover of any particular issue.

The hard part of flag design is not the nameplate but integrating all the other necessary information.

This is also the point at which, without further discussion, TimesTen became the house font—because it worked so well for the flag! In the flag it is horizontally scaled by computer to make it chunkier, with a handdrawn dot on each *i* because the computer created oval dots.

Writing
MAGAZINE

The flag of a publication is equivalent to the symbol of a corporation.

Because the flag must match the message to the market instantly, the designer should resist pressure to start work on it until the target market is clearly defined.

This is the precise point where the blue of

Publication size is usually a commercial rather than a design decision

The designer is rarely consulted about the size of a publication before it is too late to make meaningful input. An advertisement to appear in a magazine is usually a given page size or a multiple of pages or a given part of a page; in newspapers an ad is a number of standard columns wide by one of several standard heights. A flyer or a multifold brochure is usually designed to fit an economical standard paper size.

The design of a newspaper also starts with its size given, either broadsheet or half broadsheet, which we call tabloid. Size is a marketing and financial decision rather than a design one.

And the same with a magazine or a book. The magazine we are designing here had its size determined by Grant standing before a table with on his left a scale borrowed from the post office and on his right a guillotine. When a dummy magazine of the correct number of pages of the chosen paper was trimmed to a weight which fitted precisely into a postage band acceptable to David, that was the size the designer had to work in. It was 275mm high by 210mm wide.

This book you're holding in your hand, where you would expect me as the originator of the series to decide on a precise size, was in fact specified by me to the publisher only as 'A4 or your nearest standard size'. It ended up 'Hong Kong quarto', which is 240mm high by 180mm wide because the commissioning editor had done a fashion series which worked well in that size and because we already knew that to meet the proposed cover price we would

An American or British designer may work in either imperial inches or metric millimetres; many British clients still think in inches. In Europe and the Far East, only metric measurements are acceptable. Never work in points, picas, ems and ens—clients don't appreciate being baffled.
25.4mm = 1in
A4 = 210×297mm
or 8.27×11.69in
A3 = 297×420mm
or 11.69×16.54in
Letter = 8.5×11.5in
Tabloid = 17×11.5in

Three simple rules about size, orientation and bleed

be printing in the Far East.

Unless you've learned the lesson already, forget what you were taught at college about paper cost determining **bleed** and **trim sizes** or the shape of your design.

There are only three important rules about size and shape. You can't design and print larger than the largest available paper size. Never work in landscape—horizontal format—unless you have first ascertained that your client, the entire distribution chain, and over 90 per cent of your target audience will not find it objectionable for any one of a thousand possible reasons, starting with cost, storage space, handling convenience, desk space, and endlessly on and on. And, finally, less than 3mm or .125 inch of bleed will cause trouble sooner rather than later.

Bleed is printing beyond the edge of the paper so that when the publication is trimmed the printing goes all the way to the edge of the trimmed page even if the trimming is carelessly done. Obviously, when you intend bleeding print off the edge of the page, your printing page must be bigger than the trimmed size by at least 3mm all round, that is 6mm or .25 inch extra in both directions.

In the United States the largest sheet normally available is 38×50 inches. In Britain 60×40 inches, called double quad crown, is often available but the common metric standard includes BO which is 1000×1414mm or near enough 39×56 inches. Larger sizes can be obtained by special order but usually at a stiff premium.

Portrait orientation in cyan—the sea-blue colour—and **landscape** orientation in magenta—the reddish colour. Cyan, magenta, yellow and black are the colours printed by the four plates in full colour printing. Between them they make up all the colours of the rainbow.

The flag lies at the cutting edge of selling any magazine to its intended audience

The flag of the magazine or newspaper is that part of the cover which includes the nameplate, the date of issue, and often other information. It is wrong to call it the masthead, a name that should be reserved for the listing on the inside somewhere of all the editorial, legal and financial officers of the publisher.

The flag is extremely important because it carries the major burden of distinguishing the publication on the newsstand, where there will be many other publications vying for the customer's attention and money. Even a tied company newsletter has competition from everything else on the worker's desk, and should appeal for his attention accordingly.

Sprin

Writin

The flag of a publication is equivalent to the symbol of a corporation.

Because the flag must match the message to the market instantly, the designer should resist pressure to start work on it until the target market is clearly defined.

This is the precise point where the blue of

Vriting

992   From the publishers of **WRITERS** NEWS MAGAZINE

g MAGAZINE

the subscription monthly was excluded from use in the newsstand quarterly. Instead we decided not to have a house colour at all, though the blue would stay with the subscription monthly for the foreseeable future, and would be used as a mnemonic link to the sister magazine on the cover of the newstand quarterly.

Instead of a house colour, which can be limiting, we would change the outline—the red above—to suit the balance of colour on the cover of any particular issue.

The hard part of flag design is not the nameplate but integrating all the other necessary information.

This is also the point at which, without further discussion, TimesTen became the house font—because it worked so well for the flag! In the flag it is horizontally scaled by computer to make it chunkier, with a handdrawn dot on each *i* because the computer created oval dots.

The art of the cover is creativity within constraint

A common design for a magazine cover contains the flag, a single large image, a large-type plug for the best item inside, and smaller-type plugs for several next-best items. These elements are so standard that they have earned acronyms among specialist designers. The SLI is the single large image, the BCO is the big come-on or the major text plug, and the ORs or also-rans are the lesser text plugs. A smaller, secondary image is sometimes used and this is known as the kicker.

The art of cover design lies in the arrangement of these standard elements so that your magazine (or book or report or other publication) wins more than its fair share of takers—even in competition with the best work of other designers. Remember, your new cover must compete with the veteran survivors of many similar sudden death playoffs. A newsstand is the most pitiless design forum in the world: there are no second prizes and no second chances.

The cover design, like every other part of the design, arises from the practice of creativity inside the constraints imposed by the market, the medium, the available finances, and to a much lesser extent the client's personal preferences. If this last accounts for more than 5 per cent of decisions, I return the retainer and leave; every designer must decide individually when professional integrity is endangered.

There were three major considerations in designing the *Writing Magazine* cover. First, and by far the most important from the designer's viewpoint, was the bad news, brought by Grant and Richard, that we

This was the only cover photograph I would be offered for the first issue. It is of the novelist Jilly Cooper, very beautiful and instantly recognizable, but as a photograph not exactly in the David Bailey class. This is actual size and is my rough 75dpi placement scan after posterisation to eight levels per colour element to try and save the photograph.

could definitely expect no transparencies and most likely no better colour photographs than the one I was trying to reject. The publicity machine for the sort of author written about or interviewed in the magazine is not sufficiently sophisticated to do any better. The available photographs were likely to be smallish and not of very good quality. David investigated having our own photographs taken but the cost was out of proportion to the gain.

Second, the audience of writers is decidedly heterogeneous in their interests. In the room on the day we discussed this were David as a writer of railway books, Richard as a writer of textbooks, Grant as a writer for other typographers, Carol as a journalist, and me as a novelist. As writers we all had different creative problems and faced different marketing problems. The audience for the magazine would be even more diversified in its interests. Every next–best item that could find a space would therefore have to be squeezed onto the cover.

Thirdly, because of the small natural constituency for this magazine, the sudden death nature of magazine publishing was even more of a threat. We had to have a truly substantial sale for the very first issue to persuade the distribution chain that it would be profitable to support the magazine. Targeting our quarter per cent of the newsstand traffic would require very high visibility—on newsstands where every other designer was also trying for maximum visibility. When the going gets tough…

Let's tackle these constraints one by one.

The inset is a more obviously suitable picture for a magazine cover—but for a skiing or holiday magazine! Or just Ms Cooper's head, if we could enlarge it, would make a suitable single large image…but the photograph would not enlarge.

Writin

Spring 1992   From the publishers of WRITERS

1. The flag belongs at the top of the cover. Put it there. Don't waste time on clever positions.

2. The number of articles and other items to be mentioned on the cover was turned into a design feature by the box that unified them and integrated them with the flag. This box is a called a sidebar.

3. The size of the image was fixed by the need t reduce the available photograph to half-siz to ensure decent reproduction. The majo plug was laid out in the remaining space, kerned and leaded to suit. We sha come to kerning and leading

g

MAGAZINE

4. We had to turn Ms Cooper around to face into the design rather than out of it. I feared she would notice and she did. The number of colours in the photograph was reduced to 32 to make it print sharper. This version is still my rough scan; high resolution scans are usually held only by the bureau to save space on the studio hard disk. But reduced by half, it prints better than the full size copy on p30. Reduction works every time.

5. A designer choosing a dominant colour for a cover rolls the dice for high stakes. Yellow was, when I made this choice, second only to green as an 'unacceptable' colour for a magazine cover. That, anyway, was the received wisdom. But we simply had to distinguish our magazine from all the others on the rack.

Now turn the page to see how it all comes together

Writing

From the publishers of **WRITERS** NEWS

Spring 1992

£1.

FINDING YOUR PUBLISHER

A five-step guide for the first time novelist

Jilly Cooper: Paperback Polo

From here we are into the hard slog of detail work, so let's take stock. We have seen that graphic design works best when it derives functionally from the needs of the target audience. Of course, if it were truly that simple, almost anyone could do it with a reasonable expectation of success. The reality is that the distribution chain, every designer creating publications for rival marketers, and one's own accountants are all in league to trip up the careless designer.

Thus the best designer is the one who communicates most effectively in spite of all the constraints. The designer of genius is the one who makes the constraints work to achieve profitable ends.

A rival publisher described the page on your left as 'the sort of cover that grabs the money and runs.' I can't think of a higher compliment. Graphic art, which rewards creativity so highly, has nothing to do with fine art or even conventional 'good taste'; it is a branch of the communications industry.

If you think that too strong, consider the tasteful spread below. Would it, turned into a cover, have sold *Writing Magazine?*

The finished article, at 86% of full size: crude, pointed, as effective as a sledgehammer. This cover established the magazine conclusively. So many designers copied it that six months later the newsstands looked like a daisyfield. At this point Grant and I had great difficulty persuading David it was time to let the yellow go, that it no longer conferred distinction.

32

Writing

MAGAZINE

Spring 1992   From the publishers of WRITERS NEWS

1. The flag belongs at the top of the cover. Put it there. Don't waste time on clever positions.

2. The number of articles and other items to be mentioned on the cover was turned into a design feature by the box that unified them and integrated them with the flag. This box is called a sidebar.

3. The size of the image was fixed by the need to reduce the available photograph to half-size to ensure decent reproduction. The major plug was laid out in the remaining space, kerned and leaded to suit. We shall come to kerning and leading.

FINDING YOUR PUBLISHER
A five-step guide for the first-time novelist

33

Five steps from problem to profit

4. We had to turn Ms Cooper around to face into the design rather than out of it. I feared she would notice and she did. The number of colours in the photograph was reduced to 12 to make it print sharper. This version is still my rough scan; high resolution scans are usually held only by the bureau to save space on the studio hard disk. But reduced by half, it prints better than the full size copy on p30. Reduction works every time.

5. A designer choosing a dominant colour for a cover rolls the dice for high stakes. Yellow was, when I made this choice, second only to green as an 'unacceptable' colour for a magazine cover. That, anyway, was the received wisdom. But we simply had to distinguish our magazine from all the others on the rack.

Now turn the page to see how it all comes together

GRAPHIC DESIGN IN THE COMPUTER AGE   PUBLICATIONS FOR PROFESSIONAL COMMUNICATORS

Structure

The control grid is, next to movable type itself, the most useful invention in the history of graphic design.

The control grid is a graphic designer's multiplication tool. It makes every hour of the most humble DTP operator count for four, and every hour of a top designer is worth a thousand by courtesy of the grid. It helps a designer place copy precisely even on hungover mornings. It also offers the same designer immortality.

The great advantage of the grid is repeatability. Once the grid is set by the designer, huge magazines or books can be created in that image by assistants. Should the designer leave for greener pastures, the design lives on in the hands of the publisher who paid for it. The grid enables even a modestly financed publisher to call in a top designer to design a magazine, which will be made up by less exhorbitantly rewarded operators.

The graphic design control grid is the great unsung hero of our culture. Create it with care. Honour and observe it.

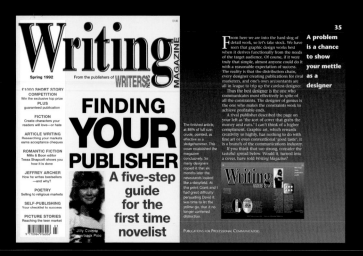

4

**Every good
design has
a grid**

At this edge you would expect the design to be flush with the edge of the cover, because the back cover is taken with an advertisement, but in fact the cover will be bigger than the page size by half the amount of foldover in cases where the magazine is stapled. In this case we allowed 3mm for foldover around 64 pages and of that allocated 1.5mm to the cover itself, so that the cover is 211.5mm trimmed size

This side the word 'MAGAZINE' sits right on the trim edge of the magazine but the colour is carried on another 3mm or .125in minimum of 'bleed' to allow for trimming—as it is on the other sides too. The green box indicates the trimmed size of the magazine. The size of the cover was laid out with its bleeds before work started. But the green grid lines were added specifically for this demonstration.

It is sometimes said, by those who have not given the matter sufficient thought, that a simple design does not need a grid. That's dangerous. Every design, no matter how simple, requires a grid. What *is* true is that for the simplest designs the designer may not find it necessary explicitly to draw the lines of an obvious grid.

In the design opposite, for instance, any designer who has to follow it would have to be blind or incompetent not to grasp instantly the implicit alignments now indicated by green lines.

But even in so simple a design I would have drawn a grid if it were not for the special circumstances of this particular design. The sound reason to draw a grid on every design is that it serves as a guide for the craftsmen who produce the publication. In this case, however, Grant Shipcott would be both designing the later covers and producing the magazine—and I knew he wouldn't do anything stupid. It cannot be stressed too much to new graphic designers and those altogether new to the graphic arts trades that almost any error anywhere in the chain of command will be laid at the designer's door. If every other excuse fails, the reason will be that 'the designer didn't make his/her intention clear.'

You can't win, so draw the grid and save yourself some tears.

Furthermore, if you are designing electronically, lock frames that should be immovable in place, and group the elements of complicated structures intelligently so that only those which require change may be ungrouped for work.

**The grid is
a guide for
associated
craftsmen
—and the
designer's
insurance
policy**

Inside the white sidebar there is an element of the grid that the designer would legitimately not show because it is automatically controlled by the spacing between lines known as the text leading.

Every good design has a grid

At this edge you would expect the design to be flush with the edge of the cover, because the back cover is taken with an advertisement, but in fact the cover will be bigger than the page size by half the amount of foldover in cases where the magazine is stapled. In this case we allowed 3mm for foldover around 64 pages and of that allocated 1.5mm to the cover itself, so that the cover is 211.5mm trimmed size

This side the word 'MAGAZINE' sits right on the trim edge of the magazine but the colour is carried on another 3mm or .125in minimum of 'bleed' to allow for trimming—as it is on the other sides too. The green box indicates the trimmed size of the magazine. The size of the cover was laid out with its bleeds before work started. But the green grid lines were added specifically for this demonstration.

£1.95

Writing
MAGAZINE

Spring 1992   From the publishers of WRITERS NEWS

£1000 SHORT STORY COMPETITION
Win the exclusive top prize
PLUS
guaranteed publication

FICTION
Create characters your readers will love—or hate

ARTICLE WRITING
Researching your markets earns acceptance cheques

ROMANTIC FICTION
Mills & Boon editor Tessa Shapcott shows you how it is done

JEFFREY ARCHER
How he writes bestsellers —and why?

POETRY
Selling to religious markets

SELF-PUBLISHING
Your checklist to success

PICTURE STORIES
Reaching the teen market

FINDING YOUR PUBLISHER

A five-step guide for the first time novelist

It is sometimes said, by those who have not given the matter sufficient thought, that a simple design does not need a grid. That's dangerous. Every design, no matter how simple, requires a grid. What *is* true is that for the simplest designs the designer may not find it necessary explicitly to draw the lines of an obvious grid.

In the design opposite, for instance, any designer who has to follow it would have to be blind or incompetent not to grasp instantly the implicit alignments now indicated by green lines.

But even in so simple a design I would have drawn a grid if it were not for the special circumstances of this particular design. The sound reason to draw a grid on every design is that it serves as a guide for the craftsmen who produce the publication. In this case, however, Grant Shipcott would be both designing the later covers and producing the magazine—and I knew he wouldn't do anything stupid. It cannot be stressed too much to new graphic designers and those altogether new to the graphic arts trades that almost any error anywhere in the chain of command will be laid at the designer's door. If every other excuse fails, the reason will be that 'the designer didn't make his/her intention clear.'

You can't win, so draw the grid and save yourself some tears.

Furthermore, if you are designing electronically, lock frames that should be immovable in place, and group the elements of complicated structures intelligently so that only those which require change may be ungrouped for work.

The grid is a guide for associated craftsmen —and the designer's insurance policy

Inside the white sidebar there is an element of the grid that the designer would legitimately not show because it is automatically controlled by the spacing between lines known as the text leading.

The designer's gift is to reduce decision making confusion to graphic clarity

It must be admitted that the cover on the previous page is a simple design. But note that it is simple because we identified only three crucial purposes for the cover and serviced these relentlessly to the exclusion of everything else. In this particular case some decisions—notably type choices—slid effortlessly into place by presumption and a minor amount of trial and error, which helped to speed the process and keep the grid simple.

Most designs have a greater number of demands and purposes—and therefore are usually more complicated. Consequently the grid is more involved, which makes an explicit and complete formal grid necessary for everyone else to follow.

In analysing the designs for the feature and service pages of *Writing Magazine* and *Writers News*, the important points for you to notice are not the actual designs but the kinds of questions asked and answered, and the order and impact of those decisions. Process over particulars!

Your answers to the questions will be different. Your design will be different. But your questions will be the same, and in roughly the same order.

An important warning: we appear to be dissecting a tidy, compartmentalized process. But decision making in any design of this magnitude is neither tidy nor compartmentalized. In particular the design of the grid progresses side by side with decisions on typefaces and styles, which we start discussing on p46.

Real-life graphic design is a high class juggling act.

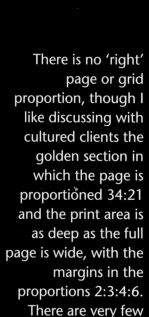

There is no 'right' page or grid proportion, though I like discussing with cultured clients the golden section in which the page is proportioned 34:21 and the print area is as deep as the full page is wide, with the margins in the proportions 2:3:4:6. There are very few jobs that can afford such elegant layout. Illustration after Jan Tschichold.

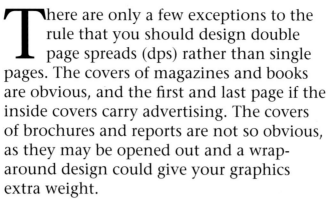

There are only a few exceptions to the rule that you should design double page spreads (dps) rather than single pages. The covers of magazines and books are obvious, and the first and last page if the inside covers carry advertising. The covers of brochures and reports are not so obvious, as they may be opened out and a wrap-around design could give your graphics extra weight.

The first grid is the **trimmed page size** with two pages side by side to make a dps.

Grid design is a simple step-by-step process

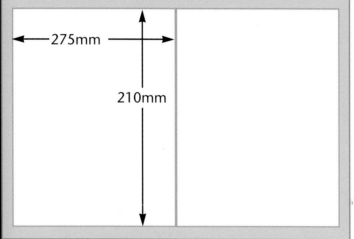

Indicate the **bleed** of 3mm or .125in on all sides where it is required. The bleed is the amount by which illustrations intended to print to the page edge are printed beyond it to allow for trimming. After this, we won't show the bleed but, if you work in traditional makeup, you should. In computerised design the exact distance of the bleed is usually irrelevant as long as it is at least 3mm, so designers simply drag the box for the illustration over the edge of the page by eye. It looks untidy but it works well enough and saves time.

Size of page after trimming is shown white with bleed area grey. Two pages side by side make a **double page spread**. It is dangerous to design on single pages. Lightly drawn pencil lines or light blue printed lines will not be picked up by the process camera.

The minimum grid contains irreducible regular items

All repetitive designs have repeating design elements and therefore repeating grid elements in the same place on all pages—or, more likely, mirrored across each spread.

Common regular elements are the **page size** and **bleed** (previous page), top and bottom **margins**, outside and inside margins, **title**, **page number**, **date**, **running head** if any. It is smart to design one **master grid** containing all these items and then to design all the other grids—plural because in a professional designer's life there are very

few publications with only a single grid—by exception to the master grid. Though I show columns here, it is usually not wise to show columns on your master grid—stick to the print area and you can then allocate columns as you please.

The space between the margins is the **print area**, which is usually taken by people in the trade to include headlines and body text but to exclude the running items. The space between the print areas is called the **gutter**. Never call the space between columns a gutter, call it **column spacing**.

It is customary for the graphic designer to show **trim marks**, which are hairlines (.25point thick) starting about a millimeter from the trim edge on all four corners of the page or spread. DTP programs add trim marks either by default or on request.

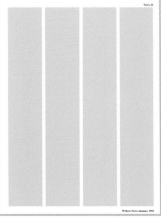

A publication usually requires at least two column widths, often more

One of the basic truisms of magazine design is that news goes on four columns and features on three or fewer—a useful cliche for any kind of publication that carries more than one kind of content. Short news pieces look bigger and more important on a narrow width that gives them depth; the narrow width adds urgency. Features and think pieces look more thoughtful and impressive on a wider measure. Up to 80 characters wide, additional width adds authority; beyond 80 characters the text is merely unreadable because the eye loses touch with it—in the jargon, the saccadic rhythm is broken.

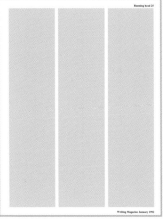

Notice how an equal print area looks urgent, even compelling, with a larger number of narrow columns, and more authoritative as well as more restful with fewer, wider columns.

And a few 'special' designs are always required

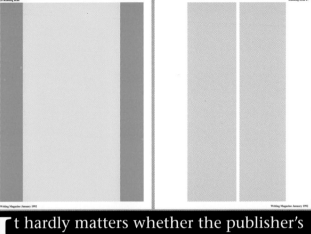

It hardly matters whether the publisher's own column is special beyond that of other contributors: if the boss is convinced it is special, the designer has to provide a special format for it. There are usually other items which require a special lift, like editorials in papers, op-ed pieces also in newspapers, and so on. My own experience is that I am usually grateful for the opportunity offered by such pages to grab back a little white space to improve the overall grey appearance of the publication.

In this instance, where we were cramming in the maximum number of words as a primary design intention, even a

Contents

PIC OF THE MAIN MAN IN THE STAR-CROSSED BOX

couple of special pages were manna from heaven. They are both on the same print area but one has standard width columns (from the 3-column page) with two sidebars, while the other uniquely has two fat columns with a single sidebar. It was intended from the beginning that illustrations could stick out into the sidebar or that it could carry captions, but would remain largely white.

Human elements must always be considered

A nother kind of special design is required for covers and section part titles, and sometimes for the service pages, like letters to the editor. My practice is to do the cover and section part titles on whichever grid is appropriate to the material in the section. The designer who puts a 3-column cover on a 4-column section misses an easy integrating device.

Note, incidentally, that we decided to keep the *Writers News* flag more or less intact. The feeling was that, considering how much else we were changing, this would be too much. A minor cleanup was all that was done. Even the PMS300 blue, which I hated, had to stay.

The contents page dummy, opposite, is on the two column plus two sidebar grid originally designed for the publisher's column. Since the designer had carelessly allocated the publisher's column style to the contents, another 'special' grid had to be devised (below, opposite) which also allowed more words.

Typography

Resist the temptation to show illustration or headline positions on the grid at this stage of its development. To integrate illustrations and headlines properly with the grid, the text face must first be chosen, together with its interline spacing or leading. But the text face is always chosen in association with the display face to be used for setting headlines and other large matter. As you can see, the process of publication design is not neatly compartmentalized.

The choice of typefaces is the most important function performed by the graphic designer. There is a school of thought which makes an arguable case that a graphic designer is merely a typographer with some additional tacked-on minor skills. Until halfway through the twentieth century graphic designers were always called typographers. Even designers destined to spend their careers in television start their training with typography because their instructors believe that the letterform is the mother of all styled communication.

5

Type selection *looks easy* but the wrong choice will destroy a design

Typeface selection is the one area where a graphic designer's client is well advised not to interfere. It is the key pressure point of any design process, and the one place where the designer is uniquely and, most often, exclusively qualified. On the selection of typefaces and their specification depends complex consequences that only a trained and experienced designer can appreciate.

On all other matters a designer may compromise with the knowledge or preference of the client. Indeed, in all other differences of opinion the graphic designer *should* compromise with the client because the client knows the target market best. But never on typography, unless the client is an experienced typographer, say the production manager of a large publisher or a senior art director at a major ad agency.

My own practice is to consider the client's typeface suggestions alongside my own. He could prove right! If his choice won't work but he insists on it, I leave.

It pays to make a rigorous attitude to type selection clear at an early stage. For instance, during preliminary talks with David Thomas he said, 'I want to keep Plantin.' Even though I knew that for a publisher he is uncommonly knowledgeable about type, I promptly stood and offered to recommend an otherwise sound designer who would take orders on type selection. David immediately agreed instead that I should consider Plantin with my own suggestions but that he would reserve the final choice to himself. *That* is a proper division of responsibilities.

Accent, capital, ascender and x heights, the baseline and descender depth. The A and the x stand on the baseline. The curves of rounded characters exceed the x-height by a small margin to make them 'look right' compared to square characters.

Type selection *looks* easy but the wrong choice will destroy a design

Typeface selection is the one area where a graphic designer's client is well advised not to interfere. It is the key pressure point of any design process, and the one place where the designer is uniquely and, most often, exclusively qualified. On the selection of typefaces and their specification depends complex consequences that only a trained and experienced designer can appreciate.

On all other matters a designer may compromise with the knowledge or preference of the client. Indeed, in all other differences of opinion the graphic designer *should* compromise with the client because the client knows the target market best. But never on typography, unless the client is an experienced typographer, say the production manager of a large publisher or a senior art director at a major ad agency.

My own practice is to consider the client's typeface suggestions alongside my own. He could prove right! If his choice won't work but he insists on it, I leave.

It pays to make a rigorous attitude to type selection clear at an early stage. For instance, during preliminary talks with David Thomas he said, 'I want to keep Plantin.' Even though I knew that for a publisher he is uncommonly knowledgeable about type, I promptly stood and offered to recommend an otherwise sound designer who would take orders on type selection. David immediately agreed instead that I should consider Plantin with my own suggestions but that he would reserve the final choice to himself. *That* is a proper division of responsibilities.

Accent, capital, ascender and x heights, the baseline and descender depth. The A and the x stand on the baseline. The curves of rounded characters exceed the x-height by a small margin to make them 'look right' compared to square charactrers.

KISS—or, keep it simple and you can't lose

Teaching typographers can make the varieties of typefaces sound more complex than the Heinz product range. In fact there are only two major typeface groups of relevance to a practising graphic designer. They are **serif** faces and **sans serif** faces, commonly referred to as serif and sans. The words are French and properly pronounced 'sir-reef' and 'sons' but 'serrif' is pretty common in the reprographic trades, so don't sweat it.

The serif is the little ear at the top and bottom of the vertical stroke of the d in the bottom group on the blue panel. Serifs are arranged on characters in three horizontal lines: on the baseline, at the top of the ascender, and at the bottom of the descender. Rounded, bowled characters like the g have serifs on the same horizontal lines as the 'straight' characters. The purpose of the serif is to guide the reader's eye along the line of text to ease reading speed and comprehension.

It is generally accepted that sans serif text, without serifs, seen top right and in this paragraph, is more difficult to read in bulk.

Back to serifs. Note that the characters in each group share certain traits such as the shape, size and placement of the bowl of rounded letters, and the position of the thicker part or **stress** of the curves. Such similarities aid the serifs in speeding the eye along the line of text.

e
c

ed

d

C

e
1

e
ed

**Sans serif is
used for
headlines,
serif for
body copy**

Everything else is merely a refinement of what you already know

But it is never quite so simple. Sans serif as a text face has its own passionate supporters, and is used by some of the the trendier magazines as 'house fonts'.

Serif faces are grouped by the shape of the serif and the direction of the stress into old face (bracketed, sloping serifs and angled stress) and modern face.

A typical modern face with thin straight serifs and vertical stress is Bodoni, first cut circa 1790. There are also the so-called Egyptienne faces or slab-serifs with straight, square-cut serifs and, usually, little or no stress so that all parts of the letterform are of equal width. They are good for posters.

A nearly obsolete group except for 'special' work is fraktur, an early face that looks like ye olde Englishe medieval font but was in everyday use in Germany well into this century. Speciality faces old or new may be interesting but are not often of use in publications and only rarely even in advertising when made by professionals.

'In typography, function is of major importance, form is secondary, and fashion almost meaningless.'
Aaron Burns

Look at the typefaces in specimen books and make up your own mind. A good font is one that you like and which works effectively to achieve your design purpose.

RUBBER STAMP
A VERY SPECIAL FACE!

Gill Sans, English sans

Zapf Chancellery, script

Rockwell, slab serif

Peignot, speciality face

𝕱𝖊𝖙𝖙𝖊, fraktur or gothic

Garamond, old face

Baskerville, transitional face

Bodoni, modern face

The grotesques, ancestors of the modern sans serif, prefigured the weight ranges in modern font families

From a working designer's viewpoint the grotesque group of faces is far more important than being able to name the minor differences between various groups of typefaces. They sound like they should look like the fraktur on p53 but in fact they are ultra-bold faces originally developed for screamer headlines on flyers and posters and in newspapers.

Their relevance to the modern designer is that they introduced the concept of graded weights which is now virtually compulsory for any newly designed sans whose designer wants to succeed. A much smaller range of weights is sometimes available for newly designed serif faces.

From a variety of weights, it was only a small step to include the other emphasis-making variation, italics, in the modern concept of a complete font.

Today any standard font consists of a medium weight with attendant bold weight plus at least an italic with its own attendant bold italic version. By the traditional way of counting that would have been four fonts. To avoid confusion, such a group is usually called a **font family**.

Many font families include lighter and/or heavier weights than the 'medium' and these are crucial to modern design practice. If you look at the cover of this book, you will find that areas of varying interest or importance are differentiated chiefly by the weight of the typeface used.

It is good practice to call the slanted version of a sans serif font an **oblique** rather than an italic as italic really refers to the handwriting-derived cursive faces.

Who could possibly ask for more than the eight levels of emphasis available in both upright and oblique versions in Neue Helvetica? A designer can. There are several widths of Helvetica too…

Neue Helvetica
Neue Helvetica
Neue Helvetica
Neue Helvetica
Neue Helvetica
Neue Helvetica
Neue Helvetica
Neue Helvetica
Neue Helvetica
Neue Helvetica
Neue Helvetica
Neue Helvetica
Neue Helvetica
Neue Helvetica
Neue Helvetica

Column width and grey appearance determines body text size

Having, in theory at least, considered all the possibilities, the designer is now in a position to choose the face which will best suit the requirements of the design.

In practice, as we have seen, most designers use sans serif for heads and serifs for body copy. A few indulge their tendency towards unrelenting modernism by using sans serif for body copy, often **reversed** out of black or coloured tints.

Only when the problem posed by the target market or the medium is exceptional will most designers vary this reflex. Two of our examples, the news and quarterly magazines, have special problems calling for special typeface consideration; that is one reason why I chose them. Our third and fourth running examples, this book and the series *Graphic Design in the Computer Age* to which it belongs, are aimed at designers and might lend themselves to treatment anywhere between the pseudo-conservative (this book until you start studying it closely) to the blatantly outrageous. Only experience helps you discriminate between those projects you can create on your reflex type preferences and those for which you must look further.

abcdefghijklmnopqrstuvwxyzabcdefghijklm
The theory is that the minimum typesize should fit one and a half alphabets into the column. That would make the type above too big for routine reading. Check—by standing back from your art or your screen and squinting your eyes—how grey your text will look when unrelieved by headlines or illustrations.

abcdefghijklmnopqrstu-
vwxyzabcdefghijklm

The theory is that the minimum typesize should fit one and a half alphabets into the column. In real life columns are made wide enough to fit one and a half alphabets at any readable size only by designers on the arty-farty fringe who will never be given a mass market design job. Everyone else chooses narrower columns and larger faces.

Start with the narrowest column and try the fonts you are considering in it, complete with their leading. Here we already arrived at a preliminary combination of 10pt type on 11pt interline spacing, that is additional leading of 1pt.

This face is Plantin, the client's lifetime favourite among types. It is a fine face but for our purposes its close cousin Times Ten, right, is superior in many technical aspects. But, mainly, on our columns Times Ten just looks better than Plantin.

abcdefghijklmnopqrstu-
vwxyzabcdefghijklm

The theory is that the minimum typesize should fit one and a half alphabets into the column. In real life columns are made wide enough to fit one and a half alphabets at any readable size only by designers on the arty-farty fringe who will never be given a mass market design job. Everyone else chooses narrower columns and larger faces.

Start with the narrowest column and try the fonts you are considering in it, complete with their leading. Here we already arrived at a preliminary combination of 10pt type on 11pt interline spacing, that is additional leading of 1pt.

This face is Times Ten, a version of Times Roman, itself descended from Plantin, optimised to 10pt use. It was chosen almost without discussion because it worked very well for the flag of the quarterly. When it was shown in this column it passed on the nod and that was it.

abcdefghijklmnopqrstu-
vwxyzabcdefghijklm

This would be extremely tiring to read for more than a couple of lines and a page of it would be most unattractively dark grey. The face, Times Ten Bold, is too dark, and there is not enough interline spacing for the type to breathe in.

abcdefghijklmnopqrstu-
vwxyzabcdefghijklm

The theory is that the minimum typesize should fit one and a half alphabets into the column. In real life columns are made wide enough to fit one and a half alphabets at any readable size only by designers on the arty-farty fringe who will never be given a mass market design job. Everyone else chooses narrower columns and larger faces.

Start with the narrowest column and try the fonts you are considering in it, complete with their leading. Here we have already arrived at a preliminary combination of 10pt type on 11pt interline spacing, that is additional leading of 1pt.

This face is Palatino, an elegant, authoritative font in which I write letters to the bank and set the annual reports of blue chip companies and other top jobs. I always consider it when conservative jobs are in hand. I don't care that it has become common since it has been given away with PostScript laser printers. Eventually the wannabee trendsetters will go away and Palatino will still be a very fine font. But here it is obviously on too narrow a column to work well.

Make life easy for everyone by designing everything else on multiples of the body text linespace

Unless you are designing a radical publication, your columns are not likely to be wider than one and one-half lowercase alphabets. If they are, check that the typesize chosen fits no more than 55 or 60 characters to the line, about ten average words per line. The absolute maximum number of characters to a line that may be read, with difficulty, is 80.

Now set up your interline spacing. In our magazine examples we decided on 10pt type on 11pt leading; the leading and the linespace must be the same if all elements are to be locked to the grid. I advise you to lock all elements to the grid, because it saves so much heartbreak, frustration and eyestrain. Traditional makeup is done on a board with blue rules where the lines will fall but on the computer it is not necessary to have the grid visible to 'snap' elements to it. Opposite the line grid is shown red.

It is now an easy matter to design headlines and illustration spaces as multiples of the line grid, in this case any number of points divisible by 11. The advantage is that you will never be left with the odd unfilled space or an element encroaching on another. In effect the grid pre-automates layout.

You are reading Stone Serif 12/14.5pt, the **sidebar captions** are set in Stone Sans Regular and Demibold 11/14.5pt, and the page numbers and page heads are set in Stone Sans Bold 18/29pt. All lock to the 14.5pt grid, so that 18pt type effectively sits on 29pt leading. All this information is contained in **styles** which in computer setting is applied by clicking a button.

This is a **sidebar** caption. It is set in Stone Sans 11/14.5pt.

Snap and lock all elements to the leading grid

bcdefghijklmnopqrstuvwxyzabcdefghijklm

This is Times Ten on the widest two column width, which comes with a single sidebar. Notice that it is wider than the theoretically permissable width for 10pt Times Ten. It would therefore, if used, be used sparingly and only for very short pieces.

bcdefghijklmnopqrstuvwxyzabcde-ghijklm

This is Times Ten on the standard three column width, which is also the width of the two columns plus two sidebars design.

Text set flush left. Used when an informal appearance is required. All paragraphs should be indented or spaced by one line (or less, which causes problems with the grid) from other paragraphs, or otherwise differentiated from the previous paragraph.

Text set justified. Used for formal, authoritative text (but never for letters!). It is almost always necessary to hyphenate text to make it fit the column width without unsightly rivers of white space between words.

It is usual to write out the text specification, starting with the body text: 10/11 Times Ten, locked to the grid, paragraphs indents 2 points, justified right, hyphenated, no more than two hyphens in a row, no word to break with fewer than three characters either left behind or carried over.'

News 35

Writers News January 1992

Display faces should be chosen according to the principle that less is more

An experienced designer is not obliged to follow the rule of thumb that sans is for headlines and serif for body copy. What happened at *Writers News* is that I looked at the Avant Garde used in the existing design, threw up my hands in horror, and dismissed several possible alternatives without either making a sample or discussing it with the client. I knew from experience that the alternatives would not suit either.

At the time, Times Ten was a brand new font for desktop computer setting. It was therefore not a conservative choice, but my intention was conservative and the effect on readers was conservative, and nothing else counts. The same applies to setting the heads in upper and lower case Times Ten.

What you should consider important here is not the choice of a 'new' face for a conservative purpose, but its effect on the intended audience. The designer, on behalf of the publisher, does not prove by these choices that the magazine shares the conservative outlook of the target audience. It is true that Times Ten, to the uninitiated, in addition all its other virtues offers the solace of the familiar. But the proof of the pudding is in what designer and publisher left out: Avant Garde, other flashy faces, mad max tricks with typography and illustrations, anything obviously radical. Restraint, by definition, is what is left out. Users of publications read between the lines: they are inordinately resistant to the artificial excitements of fancy faces when used to patch up an elementally flawed design. Less is always more.

All the typeface names are 53pt, all the descriptive text underneath each name is 17/19pt. Note how much bigger some faces appear for the same nominal size.

AVANT GARDE

is far too special to be used except in very small doses, once per page at most. Fine for flags and other logotypes

There is no law against using a serif face for display

HELVETICA

is simply too cold and clinical for what we want here. It is not for nothing that its detractors call it 'Teutonica'

FUTURA

has a good range of weights but is in the same chill class as Helvetica, lacking in human warmth

GILL SANS

is fine on bookshops, train stations and in art books but not in magazines for writers

Times Ten

Who said we cannot use a serif face for headlines? Times Ten has just the right ambience for our audience

How to create display type specs the easy way

Once the body copy has been comprehensively specified, all display faces from the smallest—a crosshead in body text—to the largest can be designed by reference to the body text grid, to which it must lock for ease of operation as well as for aesthetic reasons. In the case of the magazine examples the logical procedure has brought us to multiples of 11pt. That is the equivalent of the 14.5pt building block for this book you are reading, described on p58.

Experienced designers will not need to be persuaded that detail design proceeds best from the smallest unit upwards because they know that working from the headlines downwards wastes a great deal of time and causes frustration and mistakes.

At this point, the graphic designer in charge of the project usually has to attend

The rule of thumb in type selection is that you are permitted two of everything. Two typefaces by two sizes each by two weights for each size by two styles (plain and italic) for each weight allows for sixteen emphasis/graphic possibilities. Here the text and display face are the same but the principle still applies. It was not necessary to use all sixteen permitted variations.

36 Writing Magazine

Main heads break verra pointedly

A secondary head or a major lead may stretch down this column as far as is required, to the full depth of the column if you wish but it must not run on to a second column. A secondary head or a major lead may stretch down this column as far as is required, to the full

INTRODUCTION BY
BOB GREENE

quiock brwon fow mumps over the jumps a nonsense rhyme This dummy text for the features section.

A crosshead
The quiock brwon fow mumps over the jumps a nonsense rhyme .
This dummy text for the features see

1-line optional heading
1. Don't do this
2. Be sure to do that
3. The other is a very bad thing
4. That too
5. And another thing that can help you quite a bit
6. Yes sirree. Let me take you by the hand and lead you to Canaan
7. Don't do this. Be sure to do that instead because it works

Continued on...

One line of crosshead style head if required
•Don't do this •Be sure to do that •The other is a very bad thing •That too •And another thing •Yes sirree •Let me take you by the hand •Don't do this •Be sure to do that •The other is a very bad thing •That too •And another thing •Yes sirree •Let me take you by the hand •Don't do this •Be sure to do that •The other is a very bad thing•The other is a very bad thing •That too •And another thing •Yes sirree •Let me take you by the hand •Don't do this one •Don't do this •Be sure to do that •The other is a very bad thing to do •And another thing you could try if that doesn't work

JANE TWICE-BAERRELL

JANE CONTRIB

to the tedious administrative task of writing out, element by element, the specification of each style, as we have already done for the basic indented text paragraph. This material will eventually be gathered together in the style book that all regular publications require when more than three people are likely to work on them.

There is a shortcut but it works only with small workgroups. It is to show all elements on as few pages as will take them, and to write directly on these sample page the rules for each element as well as the permitted exceptions in its uses. Editorial and other managerial staff also find these visual examples easier to grasp and follow than a theoretical description that can only be comprehended by a trained typographer. Nearly all the display elements are illustrated left.

Managers too like to know the designer is considerate of their problems

across this gutter at least to here>>

Pull quotes may run over one or two columns but not over three, though a two column pull may be centred on three columns to break up a whole page

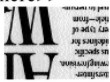

Pull quotes can run over one or two columns but not over three

The author's pic if there is one, preferably without a caption. Who else could it be? If the caption is a plug, it properly belongs in the the secondary head in the first column of the article

This two column pull quote breaks up three columns all at once but take care not to come too near side body text

De kaption over zweilinesss of kerekters. De kation over zweilinesss of kerek-ters.Denesss of kerekters

No column is to run for more than two thirds body text depth without a break

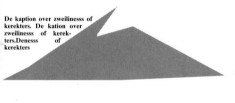

Continued from

JANE CONTRIB

If the right font is not available, have one designed

In computer setting most fonts consist merely of a group of numbers which describe a set of bezier curves forming a closed shape that is filled with colour or black. Specialist applications permit those with the necessary skills to manipulate bezier curves visually rather than as mathematical symbols, but it is always easier to start with an old-fashioned drawing—in this case done by Charles Jute on his computer—which is then electronically traced for refinement as beziers. Not a process for the fainthearted!

Everyone knows there are thousands of fonts available. If you want a set of Gaelic runes, or an Urdu font, or a set of symbols for almost any purpose, you buy it. If your needs are more special, or your client's ego so large that only a special font will soothe the savage breast, an existing font can be adapted.

Designing a whole font is a time-consuming drain on the patience of all involved, and tremendously expensive because in effect a highly paid artist will proceed for months on end by trial and error. The jargon is that font design is an iterative process, which simply means one does it over until it is right.

It is in fact the need which at first glance appears simplest, that for symbols for various odd jobs, that causes the most trouble. Here is an actual example. A client approached Grant Shipcott's X L Publishing Services to produce a plant catalogue to be mailed and sold to gardeners. A prestige, high gloss job with a large circulation, it squeezes in a great deal of information by the use of symbols to indicate species, habitats and other matters of importance to gardeners. It had for many years been set in traditional hot metal by a typesetter of the old school, now deceased; he used a hodge-podge of symbols from various fonts. No PostScript font includes symbols even approximately close to those this late printer had established as the standard, so Grant asked me to create symbols that would line up better and suit the selected font more closely. The results are shown in the white panel at the size Grant specified.

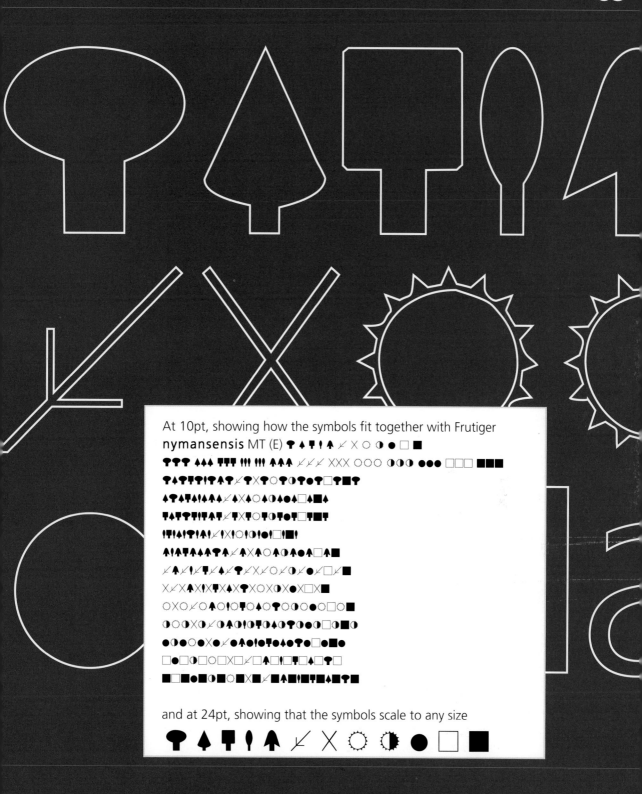

At 10pt, showing how the symbols fit together with Frutiger

nymansensis MT (E)

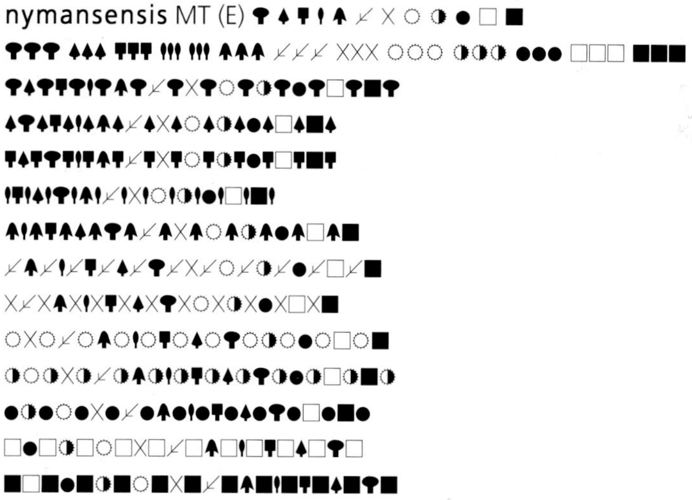

and at 24pt, showing that the symbols scale to any size

Type can be fun when you have the right message

One school of typographical thought is convinced that any manipulation of type is a betrayal of the principles of our craft. True, type manipulation done simply because the tools are available is the equivalent of smashing a Michelangelo sculpture because a hammer lies to hand. But there are exceptions.

Recognizing the rare occasion when manipulation is required to enhance the message is the art of our craft.

In Hugh Skinner's design for Apple, below, no one in the intended audience would have puzzled more than half a second over the word Multimedia.

In the fake-Futurist 'concrete poem', right, which I made for the poetry magazine published by a young friend, the manipulation is integral with the message— in fact it carries most of the message.

REVERSED

typography 101 by andré jute

Mary had a little la m b

Its fleece was m as snow

love N PERSPECTIVE

1492 falling off the edge

CHEESE

FROMAGE

HOMAGE

SQUEEZED

off the edge of the world 1992

Forever

No typographer's education is ever completed. The best designers are those who learn something new about their craft every day. And the bedrock of their craft is the letterform.

This book is about the whole publication, so we have merely touched on the art of typography. The great designers are distinguished by knowing much more of the minutiae of the letterform and its application, indeed by being obsessive about it. A good place to extend or refresh your knowledge is *Typography* by Grant Shipcott, also in this series. You already know Grant: he is the production manager and typesetter on the two magazines we are using as extended examples.

We now turn to the layout of the publication. 'Layout' is designer's shorthand for how the typography is arranged and, more, how it meshes with the other graphic elements found in any publication: lines, pictures whether illustrations or photographs, and of course colour when it is available.

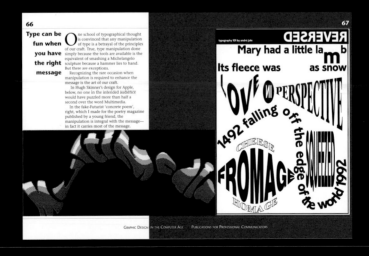

6

Layout

71

Generally speaking, we have so far avoided theoretical discussion in favour of the practical question: 'What demands are made on the designer by the client or the job, how should the designer respond, and why?'

It will not have escaped you that a great deal of the 'why' is inspired and driven by the need visually to integrate *all* elements of the publication. This is of course true for all publications, but easier to do for small, instantly grasped publications such as a single page or double page spread advertisement. Paradoxically, for the largest possible publications, encyclopædia, it is also reasonably easy to keep the whole integrated because the designer is solely in charge of the layout and the make-up. Magazines are in practice far more difficult to integrate properly but not only because so much of such variant character has to be fitted in. What makes magazines extremely difficult to keep integrated is that so much happens over such a short period when they are being put together.

The computer in the hands of journalists without design training has not helped. To a small extent a designer with management clout can ameliorate this problem by insisting that writers write and graphic designers design, but an accommodation with the computer will take years to work out; the problem is likely to become worse before we solve it.

One result of these considerations of integration is that the designer should resist 'making a sample' of any part of the inside of the magazine until the whole is designed.

Integration is a human problem as much as a graphic one

The contents page (shown at 80 per cent full size) could only be designed once the whole magazine was specified. It is on the two column plus two-sidebar grid. Nothing looks more amateur than a magazine with important pages which are at odds with the general conception by not following its grids.

Contents

Spring 1992
Vol 1 No 1

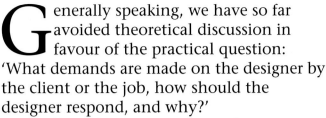

Integration is a human problem as much as a graphic one

Generally speaking, we have so far avoided theoretical discussion in favour of the practical question: 'What demands are made on the designer by the client or the job, how should the designer respond, and why?'

It will not have escaped you that a great deal of the 'why' is inspired and driven by the need visually to integrate *all* elements of the publication. This is of course true for all publications, but easier to do for small, instantly grasped publications such as a single page or double page spread advertisement. Paradoxically, for the largest possible publications, encyclopædia, it is also reasonably easy to keep the whole integrated because the designer is solely in charge of the layout and the make-up. Magazines are in practice far more difficult to integrate properly but not only because so much of such variant character has to be fitted in. What makes magazines extremely difficult to keep integrated is that so much happens over such a short period when they are being put together.

The computer in the hands of journalists without design training has not helped. To a small extent a designer with management clout can ameliorate this problem by insisting that writers write and graphic designers design, but an accommodation with the computer will take years to work out; the problem is likely to become worse before we solve it.

One result of these considerations of integration is that the designer should resist 'making a sample' of any part of the inside of the magazine until the whole is designed.

The contents page (shown at 80 per cent full size) could only be designed once the whole magazine was specified. It is on the two column plus two-sidebar grid. Nothing looks more amateur than a magazine with important pages which are at odds with the general conception by not following its grids.

The dummy is a worthwhile exercise for everyone involved but watch that many hands don't make a mess

Resist requests for sample pages out of order. Try instead to do a *complete* **dummy**, which is much more useful for everyone, including editorial, advertising, management and production people—not to mention that the graphic designer requires it for his own peace of mind.

The designer must still work out a large number of individually small but collectively ruinous problems with the publication. These problems will appear only when work starts on the layout, and with a real publication that is far too late to find and test solutions. The dummy is therefore a publication for which real copy is written by real writers, edited by real editors, typeset by real typesetters, and laid out by a real makeup artist under the watchful eye of the actual designer, after which real film is made and a real if very short press run is printed for use by the distributors, advertising department, publicity people and the publisher.

Problems discovered are fixed right there. Specifications which require refinement or other alterations are modified on the spot. The dummy also throws up the hundred-and-one small and large elements that should have been designed but were not—and are now all required within the hour.

This is normally a time of high pressure—it is the last time you can make major changes because the very next issue will appear on the newsstands. Since no one should be

Two hyphens in a row are acceptable, three are not. Capitalized words, especially proper names, should preferably not be hyphenated. It is permissable to space words to fit the line length but not to insert extra space between characters.

It is essential that justified textual material is typeset with hyphenation & letterspacing applied according to a definite predetermined and consistently applied scheme, otherwise anomalies and unattractive white spaces will occur irregularly.

This is standard or default hyphenation available in most DTP programs. Wordspacing is good and tight but five hyphens in a row is appalling!

For good colour and general appearance look first to your H&J specs

It is essential that justified textual material is typeset with hyphenation and letterspacing applied according to a definite predetermined and consistently applied scheme, otherwise anomalies and unattractive white spaces will occur irregularly.

If manual hyphenation were out of the question, this would be the best compromise for these columns with this typesize.

permitted to make any changes without the chief designer's specific consent, the pressure is greatest on the designer. It really does help if you can manage to keep your temper.

If you can, start by laying out a page with your narrowest columns because these are the trickiest to get right. What works for narrow columns will usually also work for wider columns. Not one of the specifications shown here would pass muster in a teaching institution but that is precisely what a designer is paid for, to reconcile impossible demands.

It is essential that justified textual material is typeset with hyphenation and letterspacing applied according to a definite predetermined and consistently applied scheme, otherwise anomalies and unattractive white spaces will occur irregularly.

This is what we specified for *Writers News*, shown *before manual hyphenation was applied*. Not everyone can afford manual hyphenation.

It is essential that justified textual material is typeset with hyphenation and letterspacing applied according to a definite predetermined and consistently applied scheme, otherwise anomalies and unattractive white spaces will occur irregularly.

This is a reasonable specification, but that would only become clear after manual hyphenation.

It is essential that justified textual material is typeset with hyphenation and letterspacing applied according to a predetermined and consistently applied scheme, otherwise anomalies and unattractive white spaces will occur at irregular intevals.

This is what we specified for *Writers News*, shown *after routine manual hyphenation was applied*.

Politics is the art of...

Compromise is a graphic art. The designer applies creativity to the art and psychology to the market. But only if the client is a robot are there no politics involved. Here are two related examples, on this spread a minor example of how personalities can be made to work to achieve whatever the designer considers necessary for good design, the second (overleaf) a far more serious example of the circumstances under which a designer should remember that every other member of the team is more important.

For the captions under illustrations I

This caption is justified but not written to measure so it sets badly when viewed as a graphic element.

This caption is justified and is written to measure so it sets quite well when viewed as a graphic element rather than exclusively as a text.

This caption is centred and therefore sets well as a graphic element.

Besides setting well as a graphic element, a centred caption has the advantage that, the longer it is, the more beneficially it distributes the available white space. Furthermore it saves time in make-up because it requires no manual hyphenation.

wanted to centre and float the text to make the most of the small amount of available white space. David wanted captions squared up flush, because white space seems to him paper he pays for and his designer 'wastes'; he honestly believes his readers share this view. In a meeting with half a dozen people present I therefore told editor Richard Bell he would have to write all captions to measure, adding: 'Advertising copywriters do it a hundred times a day.' His crisp response: 'I'm not an advertising copywriter!' David immediately decided it was not a battle worth fighting.

But not on vertically justified text!

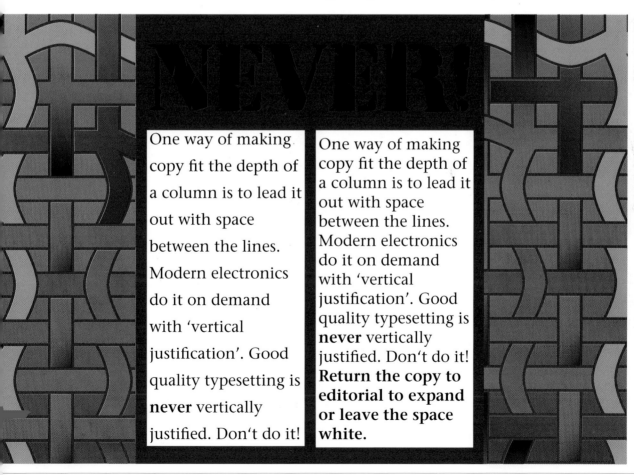

One way of making copy fit the depth of a column is to lead it out with space between the lines. Modern electronics do it on demand with 'vertical justification'. Good quality typesetting is **never** vertically justified. Don't do it!

One way of making copy fit the depth of a column is to lead it out with space between the lines. Modern electronics do it on demand with 'vertical justification'. Good quality typesetting is **never** vertically justified. Don't do it! **Return the copy to editorial to expand or leave the space white.**

Creative people are supposed to be sensitive

Richard wanted the capability of long explanatory headlines. No problem. Each article would simply start on a spread with the head across both pages.

But when Richard wanted only a short head, the result was graphically unpleasing. To 'stop the holes' I invented pictographs to sit at each end of the heads. These would be used consistently with each type of article and would help readers find precisely the kinds of articles they were interested in.

Richard disliked the pictographs intensely on the grounds that they were at odds with the spirit of a magazine for writers. I argued

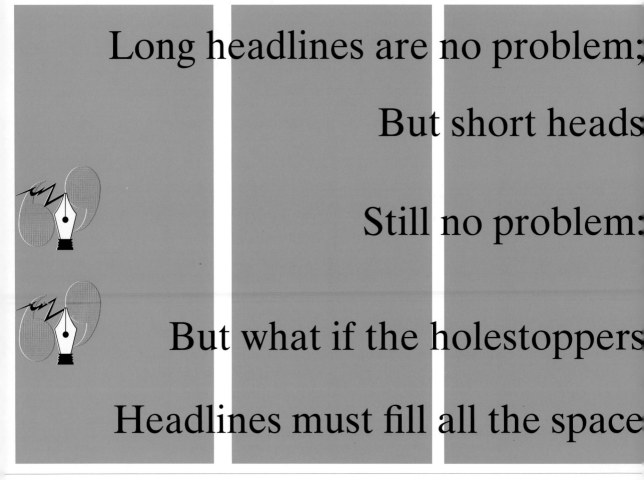

Long headlines are no problem;

But short heads

Still no problem:

But what if the holestoppers

Headlines must fill all the space

that, in addition to stopping the holes, the pictographs would guide readers to their favourite articles. Every decision-maker but Richard agreed with me. But, once I was convinced Richard would not change his mind, I dropped the idea between breakfast and lunch one day in return for a promise that Richard would write the heads to fill the space. Compare that with his attitude to writing picture captions to measure!

In a situation like this, the designer may have the votes and win the battle, but the editor (or any other important staff member) will eventually win the war.

Don't win battles only to lose the war

'ust split them across a double page

ook stupid

stop the holes!

don't appeal to the editor?

to halfway across the far columns

Kerning to give characters a better 'fit'

A problem with all display faces is that their designers gave their characters 'average' proximity to each other in the hope of being all things to all designers. The predictable upshot is that almost no designer is satisfied with the standard **kerning** of almost any font at almost any size over twelve points. Below, the 132pt Times Ten Roman has had 20 units of space removed between the A and the v, and 10 units between all other pairs of characters. This process is called kerning and many designers think a sound command of kerning the mark of a mature designer.

Average

Average

word & pictures

writing for television

B y now you will have noticed that at the dummy stage the designer considers everything, including text, first as a graphic device, asking if it integrates and contributes to the appearance of the publication.

The dummy is likely to throw up further requirements for illustrations. Left and below are more of the pictographs Vicky Squires drew for use in *Writing Magazine* as headline stoppers.

Note that if a designer orders illustrations and they are not used, they must still be paid for.

Everything that prints is a graphic

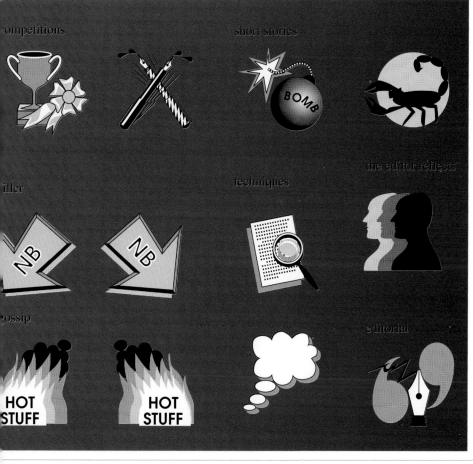

competitions

short stories

filler

techniques

the editor reflects

gossip

editorial

HOT STUFF

HOT STUFF

The most interesting graphic elements are usually bought in

When, rarely, a full studio with many designers, each specializing in a separate skill, is available, most or all the work can be done in-house. In theory the chief designer might also once in a blue moon have enough time personally to do a good part of the illustrative work, but in practice it rarely happens.

The pictographs were wanted within twenty-fours on a day when there were severe demands on my time from other directions. I was fortunate that Vicky agreed to do them within the time. We then further abused her good nature by demanding continuation notices,

Continued from ➤ p22 somehow overlooked before, in another twenty-four hours, and for good measure threw in a design Continued on... ➤ p88 for the separate contents listing for the news pages on which we decided at a very late stage. The page numbers on the contents list and the continuation notices are self-updating when moved from page to page.

Because of time problems like these, the chief designer is usually limited to drawing the more routine (but too important to be described as dull) graphics like the vertical rules separating columns and the horizontal rules separating articles or used to demarcate pages. Here we show a hairline (.25 pt) and a 1pt rule. The coloured stars are 2pts. Many attractive decorative rules are available but currently they are considered old fashioned.

Even the lead designer might become lucky and design a dogear banner!

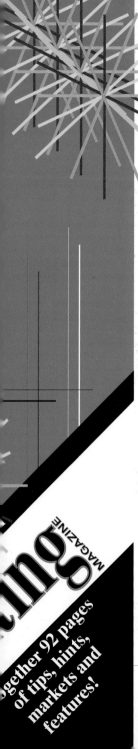

On the part-titles and elsewhere in this book are reduced examples of some of its pages to save you the bother of propping it up and stepping back to judge the layout. We shall also meet sixteen spreads from each of two other books in *Graphic Design in the Computer Age*. Each designer was given an absolutely free hand for the inside of the book with the single restraint of page size. They could bleed off all four sides of every page, use any colour, apply any graphic or production trick their heart desired. What you must judge is how well they met the challenges. As an exercise you might try to deduce the problems from the solutions. Another good exercise is to guess at the target market of a design.

Among other felicities, note how both the designers featured adhere to the grid until there is an overwhelming benefit in stepping outside it. And note that Vicky Squires in her book *Illustration* uses sans serif for body copy: for the

really experienced designer there are no rules except those dictated by experience.

If you think you have problems, consider Hugh Skinner's dilemma: his entire stock of source material for his book *Videographics* was in the proportion 4:3, but the page of the book was 3:4. Not only that—in a 2D book he lost the entire third dimension of time. He solved the problem by varying the size of his illustrations to express flow.

Creativity within restraint is gained only by genius or experience

Overleaf: 16 spreads chosen at random from *Videographics* by Hugh Skinner. Later there are more such reduced spreads from another book for you to study the layout variations and solutions.

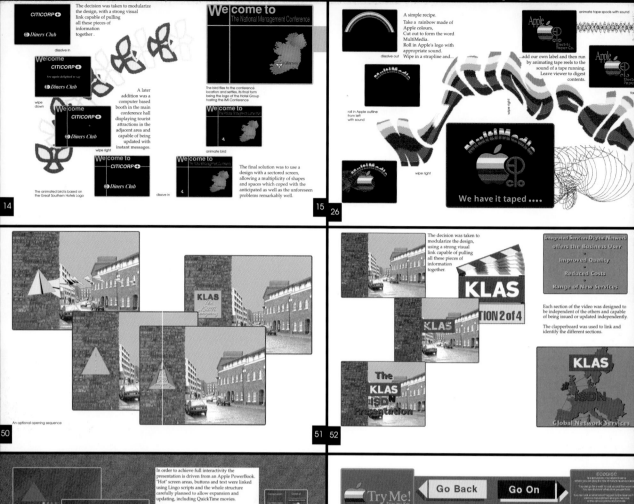

The decision was taken to modularize the design, with a strong visual link capable of pulling all these pieces of information together.

A later addition was a computer based booth in the main conference hall displaying tourist attractions in the adjacent area and capable of being updated with instant messages.

The animated bird is based on the Great Southern Hotels Logo

The bird flies to the conference location and settles, its final form being the logo of the Hotel Group hosting the IMI Conference.

The final solution was to use a design with a sectored screen, allowing a multiplicity of shapes and spaces which coped with the anticipated as well as the unforeseen problems remarkably well.

A simple recipe.
Take a rainbow made of Apple colours.
Cut out to form the word MultiMedia.
Roll in Apple's logo with appropriate sound.
Wipe in a strapline and...

...add our own label and then run by animating tape reels to the sound of a tape running. Leave viewer to digest contents.

We have it taped ....

An optional opening sequence

The decision was taken to modularize the design, using a strong visual link capable of pulling all these pieces of information together.

Each section of the video was designed to be independent of the others and capable of being issued or updated independently.

The clapperboard was used to link and identify the different sections.

Integrated Services Digital Network offers the Business User
• Improved Quality
• Reduced Costs
• Range of New Services

The KLAS ISDN Presentation

KLAS ISDN — Global Network Services

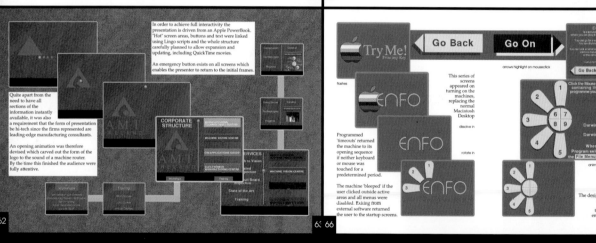

In order to achieve full interactivity the presentation is driven from an Apple PowerBook. "Hot" screen areas, buttons and text were linked using Lingo scripts and the whole structure carefully planned to allow expansion and updating, including QuickTime movies.

An emergency button exists on all screens which enables the presenter to return to the initial frames.

Quite apart from the need to have all sections of the information instantly available, it was also a requirement that the form of presentation be hi-tech since the firms represented are leading-edge manufacturing consultants.

An opening animation was therefore devised which carved out the form of the logo to the sound of a machine router. By the time this finished the audience were fully attentive.

CORPORATE STRUCTURE

Try Me! Press any key

Go Back   Go On

arrows highlight on mouseclick

This series of screens appeared on turning on the machines, replacing the normal Macintosh Desktop

Programmed 'timeouts' returned the machine to its opening sequence if neither keyboard or mouse was touched for a predetermined period.

The machine 'bleeped' if the user clicked outside active areas and all menus were disabled. Exiting from external software returned the user to the startup screens.

Click the Mouse on the white area containing the number of the programme you want to explore.

ECODISC
Sim City
Ecology
Discovery
Sim Earth
Darwins Dilemma
MacGlobe
Darwins Dilemma
MacGlobe

When in a Game or Program select Quit under the File Menu to return here

The design has been exten... by adding additi... buttons in the ce... to access the resu... environmental surv...

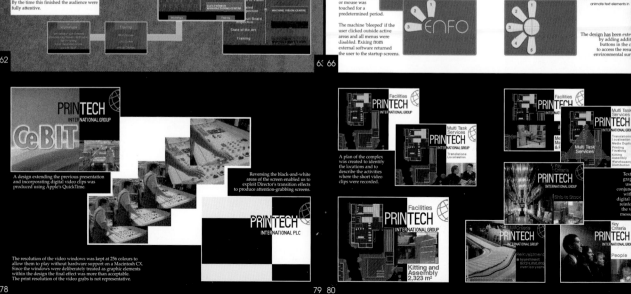

A design extending the previous presentation and incorporating digital video clips was produced using Apple's QuickTime.

Reversing the black-and-white areas of the screen enabled us to exploit Director's transition effects to produce attention-grabbing screens.

The resolution of the video windows was kept at 256 colours to allow them to play without hardware support on a Macintosh CX. Since the windows were deliberately treated as graphic elements within the design the final effect was more than acceptable. The print resolution of the video grabs is not representative.

A plan of the complex was created to identify the locations and to describe the activities where the short video clips were recorded.

Kitting and Assembly 2,323 m²

f you have o vote.....you ave no voice ...and no say n how your ountry is overned.....

......to make sure **your** voice is heard, make sure **you're** on the register

Make sure you are on the **Register**

Check at your Local Post Office or Garda Station

Department of the Environment
Register of Electors
20 Second TVC
No Voice

.....Don't be a member of the " **silent** majority !!!"

The brief required that a cycling demonstration of "Apple's Advantage" run on their current range of machines - all of which were on display- and also form the basis for an animated slide show to accompany a seminar presentation.

Intuitiveness

The Apple Advantage

The Apple Advantage

EPCo. designed the "Tick" which provided the graphic theme for Apple's stand and other exhibition material.

The photograph of the desk contains elements which fade to their equivalents on the Macintosh desktop.

Simulation is one of the great strengths of videographics.

The software interface shown here was still in the early stages of design.

Nevertheless by using computer animations we were able to create a realistic simulation of the final product and its functions.

KLAS

SHIFT
KLAS
SATIRE

Sound And Test Integrated Recording Environment

Screen Handling ISDN File Transfer

User A
ISDN
User B
SHIFT

KLAS

The secret of cost effective migration to ISDN is planning and preparation

KLAS can help you gain the competitive

The time for planning your ISDN strategy is NOW

your ISDN strategy

Later sections use video grabs from tapes shot on the premises, showing company directors and personnel with whom clients will be familiar.

TRINTECH Off-Line
KAUF 100.00

TRINTECH Off-Line
KAUF 100.00
Press

The final files were linked using Lingo scripts and then recorded onto VHS tape in PAL format using a TruVision NuVista card and an Encoder/Decoder to convert the Mac RGB signal to composite video.

This was played as a continuous information sequence at the Hanover CEBIT Exhibition to explain the sequence of entering, verifying, transmitting and updating information.

TRINTECH GUTSCHRIFT
PASSWORT:
ENTER MERCHANT PASSWORT

TRINTECH Off-Line
KARTE DURCHZIEHEN

Acting as attention grabber, the globe in Printech's logo is bounced in at the start of the cycle and as each aspect of the companies service is ticked off it is accompanied by a melodious chime.

Client company logos were used since they are instantly recognizable.

DataEase INTERNATIONAL

IBM PRINTECH INTERNATIONAL PLC

Bitstream CLARIS ORACLE

LOCATION EXPERIENCE STRUCTURE

CHECKLIST FOR EUROPE

PRINTECH INTERNATIONAL PLC

PRINTECH INTERNATIONAL PLC
Multi-Task Software Servicing
CHECKLIST FOR EUROPE
SAVINGS

ITD

Our Network

Our Network

Our Network

In each stage of this Section using the recurse points an apple will provide detailed

Brendan Whelan
General Manager

Management

Tim Walsh Eddie Moroney Dave Lombard

Ger Moffatt John Doody

Maura McGrath

Go Back Click on a Card Continue

Bank of Ireland

Bank of Ireland

e original mmission consisted of eries of cycling sections running on an pple Macintosh, giving details on the rmation Technology Department, its vices and key members of staff together th a Mission Statement.

e interactive section was then developed to provide re detailed information on staff structures and responsibilities.

solve the problem of providing considerable amounts information on large departments, the development of an entity Card' button proved a very useful graphic device.

Eddie Moroney
Head of Technology Delivery

Go Back Click on a Card Continue

Graphics were created to work in both 256 and 16 colours, since this course was designed to be used in both Windows and Macintosh environments.

Intro Level 2

Backgnd Erase classroom

Information Systems & Support

This commission involved the programming and graphic design for an interactive module to introduce beginners to computers.

It is part of a European project funded under the FORCE programme and will be distributed on compact disk in a multilanguage version.

Classroom & People Level 5

The dummy is your last chance to reassign space

By all means show your client only the most stylish pages—but do your own work on the toughest pages. Of course information/service spreads are a pain but they are also the ones which require the designer's skills more than the wide open lead features which even the prentice paste-up person can put right. The spread below offered me an opportunity to tell the layout people never to return short pieces to

---

Market index: writing for the range of horse and pony magaz

There is a wide range of horse interest titles on the market, many aimed at a young audience

When I was a pony-mad teenager, you could count the number of equestrian publications on one hand. *Riding* magazine and the now defunct *Light Horse* for adults, *Pony* magazine for children, and the news weekly, *Horse and Hound*.

Twenty-something years later, the writing rider is spoilt for choice with a wide range of titles to suit all age groups, budgets and areas of interest. As well as the general horsey publications, there are a number of specialist titles dealing with everything from eventing to carriage driving, polo to Pony Club.

As with any specialist market, you do need to know your horses. You will stand little chance of selling a technical article on riding or horse management unless you are highly experienced and your facts are absolutely watertight. But many titles also offer scope for personality interviews, humour, and other horse-related features.

Two of the bestselling general equestrian titles – *Your Horse* for adults, and *Horse and Pony* for younger riders, are published by EMAP Pursuit.

Your Horse is the largest selling monthly equestrian magazine with a circulation of 38,216 and a readership of over 100,000. Its readers are almost all female, with an average age of 29 and a 100% interest in horses. The majority of them are horse owners, throughout all levels, so the emphasis is on practical advice for owners and riders. Lots of sensible, down-to-earth help for DIY horse enthusiasts on a budget.

Editor Lesley Eccles likes prospective contributors to ring up or write, telling her a bit about themselves and detailing a couple of ideas. Include cuttings of published work if possible. If you have not been publishes, submit your article written in the style you think is suitable for *Your Horse*.

Writing Magazine Spring 1992

'Quite a lot of our features are written in-house, so we prefer freelance contributors who can offer something more offbeat – riding the Grand Canyon perhaps or, quite recently, a really humorous account of someone learning to ride. Old chestnuts need to be written in a way which is interesting and new.' Photographs are usually taken by staff photographers.

Horse and Pony, from the same stable, is the second biggest equestrian title on the market and the only fortnightly. Circulation is almost 51,000, 98% female with, again, a 100% interest in horses.

The majority of buyers are aged between 11 and 17, with the average age between 12 and 15. About half of them have a horse or pony of their own, and a large majority look after a horse.

Jenny Club in the editorial office said they use very little freelance material. The magazine has two staff writers who handle most of the practical features. A new slot, the pony photostory, is also being written by regular contributors.

However there is always room for ideas, preferably for features that are light-hearted and short. Remember, the average reader is aged 12 and does not want to concentrate on large chunks of text. So if you think you have something original to offer this type of reader, phone *Horse and Pony's* editorial team or write in.

Pony, from publishers D.J. Murphy,

is another title for the young rider. It is also one of the oldest established equestrian publications. One of my first ever sales was a short story to *Pony* in the mid 1970s, but as editor Kate Austin pointed out, the style of the magazine has changed dramatically over the years.

'We get loads of short stories sent in, but many of them are far too old-fashioned,' she explained. 'They are written by older people describing the sort of pony activities they enjoyed when they were young. But circumstances have changed.

'A lot of young riders today live in urban areas and do not necessarily have horsey parents. Very few of them grow up with the traditional Pony Club mums who feature so largely in older pony stories. A lot of adults write what I call 'cute' stories. I do not want them to be miserable and gloomy, but they must be realistic.'

Pony publish one short story of about 1200 words in each issue. There is also a wealth of instructional articles, which require good in-depth knowledge, such as information on feeding your pony, handling youngsters, and health care.

Pony's adult stable companion is *Horse and Rider*, which covers all aspects of riding and horse management. Current circulation is 38,500, with a readership of around 260,000. The vast majority are horse owners, most of them caring for their own animal, and many compete in a wide vari-

ety of equestrian events. Age range, late teens up.

Editor Alison Bridge aims to make *Horse and Rider* more in-depth than competitive titles, especially the instructional riding features which are very popular.

'We try to do new things,' she told me. 'Different ways of doing things,

Market addresses

Your Horse, EMAP Pursuit, Bretton Court, Bretton, Peterborough PE3 8DZ Tel: 0733 264666; Editor: Lesley Eccles.
Horse and Pony, EMAP Pursuit (as above); Editor: Sarah Haw.
Pony, D.J. Murphy Ltd, 296 Ewell Road, Surbiton, Surrey KT6 7AQ Tel: 081-390 8547; Editor: Kate Austin.
Horse and Rider, D.J. Murphy (as above); Editor: Alison Bridge.
Riding, Scott Publications Ltd, Corner House, Foston, Grantham NG32 2JU Tel: 0400 82032; Editor: Helen Scott.
Horse and Hound, IPC Magazines, King's Reach Tower, Stamford Street, London SE1 9LS Tel: 071-261 6315; Editor: Michael Clayton.
Eventing, Haygreen Publishing Ltd, North Street, Stoke-sub-Hamdon, Somerset TA14 6PX Tel: 0935 825210; Editor: Janet Hill.
Hurlingham Polo & Horse Review, 13 Kings Meadow, Ferry Hinksey Road, Oxford OX2 0DP Tel: 0865 883481; Editor: William Loyd.
Carriage Driving and **Pony Club**, EPG Publications Limited, Finlay House, Southfields Road, Kineton Road Industrial Estate, Leamington Spa CV33 0IH (Tel: 0926 817848).

whether stable management, feeding, health or whatever. Keeping horses has developed like anything else and there have been a lot of new ideas over the last few years which have changed the rules somewhat.'

Alison would rather see ideas than finished features. Samples of work too, please. Most of the stable management features are commissioned out to experts, similarly veterinary topics, but that does not mean these areas are sewn up. If you are an expert yourself, with something new to say – physiotherapy or acupuncture for horses, for example – then do get in touch.

The weekly magazine *Horse Hound*, published by IPC, has reputation for providing up minute news of equestrian e hunting reports, bloodstock sale dates, showjumping, and so on.

Editor Arnold Garvey advised th do have a network of correspo throughout the country, but are happy to hear from potential co lance opportunities.

From general riding maga turned to some of the more spe titles. *Eventing* is the only ma worldwide, that is exclusively to the sport of horse trials. No seventh year of publication, it is subscription through the newst over 30 countries throughout the Eventing riders are primarily between 18 and 40, both ma female.

Each issue contains authc articles on current affairs and pe ity profiles, as well as compre event reports. Champion rider Green was appointed editorial tant in 1989.

An editorial spokesman told magazine is always open to ide freelance equestrian writers. reports are largely sewn up, bu ality pieces are always p Freelances stand more chance o their work in print during the months when the eventing se over and there are fewer ev cover. Send ideas and cuttings t

---

editorial for filling out with body copy. Instead they were to leave the **end-space** blank or use a **pull-quote** to pad out text. In order to avoid editors trying to stuff in something more, I then negotiated with editorial that pull quotes could be drawn without consultation from the text at the setting/make-up stages. A one column pull quote is shown below on the final page; note the exception to the long-head rule.

Article Writing 61

llian Thornton:
n early sale to
ony magazine

Hill.

lly I looked at *Hurlingham Polo Horse Review*, a sumptuously publication which is now pub-every other month and is avail-through major newsagents. ation is now 25,000 copies per nd all polo players automatically be to the magazine.

or William Loyd has tailored the ine's contents in response to lerable reader need and d'. It now regularly covers event-unting, racing, dressage, show g and carriage driving, in addi-polo. He prefers to be contacted ideas rather than finished cripts – as much to save your s his own.

r base line, which is polo, is well after,' he told me. 'We have ed the market with the polo s, but if someone has a novel r, for instance, sees polo played ut-of-the-way place such as the ines which we may not cover ves, then we would like to hear nem.

ecent issue carried features on nporary equestrian artists, a day life of racehorse trainer Roger on, and the future of the Olympic Day Event, as well as a number reports and related features. ■

Writing Magazine Spring 1992

---

64 Profile

My writing day

For the biographer of King Henry's wives, the writing day is two hours each evening

My writing day is actually very short. Since I began writing as a professional in 1987, I have devoted approximately two hours each weekday evening to my work. This may not sound a great deal but in fact it is ideal for me because, firstly, I can estimate almost exactly how much I am going to get done, and sec-ondly, it is as much time as I can com-fortably manage after a day's teaching and looking after my two children. Also, it always leaves me on a high eager to

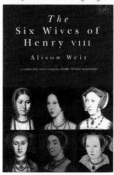

Random Century have issued
Six Wives in their Pimlico
paperback series at £10

continue my task the next evening (so much so that I am mentally planning and writing throughout each day). Writing, to me, is the perfect escape from the pressures of everyday life. When I am writing I am in another world.

My first book was 22 years in the making. Entitled *Britain's Royal Families*, it is a genealogical history of British royalty from Saxon times to the present day, presented in chronological order. Although I began collating this work in 1965, it was originally compiled for my personal use only as an informa-tion base for other books. My royal data was collated into a manual with each royal personage's genealogical details listed in alphabetical order; over the years this work was revised about seven time as more information came to hand. It was only in 1987 that it occurred to me that other people might be glad of such a reference book and I began reorganising it into something more accessible to the general reader. Hence its appearance in printed form in chronological order, a transformation that posed enormous problems not only for me but also for my editor, copy editor and the printers!

Then came *Henry's Wives* and for two years now I have been preparing a third book: *The Princes in the Tower*, a sub-ject I find most compelling. Again, the

'I always set myself a time scale'

work is based on original sources, and I have found that the truth behind the mystery has emerged with striking clar-ity during the collation of those sources into chronological order. So what is the truth? (I hope I can hear someone ask-ing!) I am not telling: you will have to wait until the autumn when the book comes out. One thing is certain: it will be controversial, something I personally rather shrink from. I did not set out to evolve a contentious theory: I set out to find the truth, and I believe I have done so.

When researching my books and dealing with so many extracts copied at flying speed from contemporary sources, I have to ensure that each item is collated in its proper place and given a code number. I then compile a list of topics to be covered in the book, and enter the code numbers by each. The information on each topic is then sifted and reorganised. This is the stage at which the pattern of the book emerges as the selected information is collated into a master plan. It is often surprising what emerges at this point: certain theo-ries have to be discarded because they are chronologically impossible, and cer-tain facts become obvious. This has hap-pened most strikingly with *The Princes in the Tower*, a book that virtually 'wrote

Photo: Kew Stark

Alison Weir:
prepares
a master plan

itself' once the facts were arranged in the right order.

Once the master plan is finished, the book is in draft. At this stage I prepare a detailed plan for submission to the pub-lishers, so that both they and I know what the finished work will be like. On the strength of this, the book is commis-sioned.

Using the master plan I then write the book in long hand. Many people have nagged me to get a word-processor but I am more comfortable with traditional methods of crafting a book. I always set myself a time scale by which to complete the book, and aim to write a chapter a week. Once the manuscript is written I type it up at a rate of ten pages a night. This way I can ensure that the finished book is delivered on time. I always use a diary and checklist for this purpose; if you deliver late, you cannot complain if your publisher fails to publish on the agreed date.

This may seem a cumbersome way of writing a book, but it works for me because it ensures that I study and eval-uate the source material and my own interpretation of it no less than five times before I deliver a work that I am satisfied is as accurate as I can make it. I also believe that, as far as possible, the subject you choose to write about should be one about which you are enthusiastic; the words will then, as my agent said when he had seen my proposal for *The Princes in the Tower*, 'leap from the page'. ■

Writing Magazine Spring 1992

Make your most critical specs visible!

It is absolutely essential that all parties, but especially editorial people, are aware of how wide/deep any illustration may be. They require this information for copyfitting and the rest of the workers in the make-up and reproduction chain will not know unless you tell them.

Rather than specify such matters in words, I like to show the dimensions on an actual page, with a description if necessary. The editor can then hold the photograph to be used next to the nearest permissable size and decide how it should be reduced or cropped to suit.

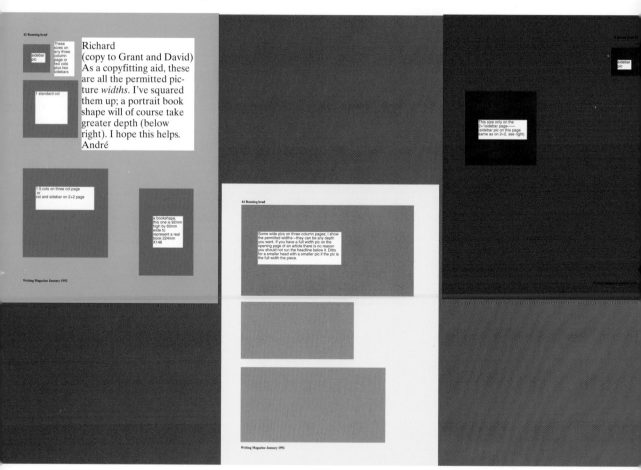

I t is illegal to use an illustration without the permission of its owner. There is a presumptive legal right to intellectual and creative ownership of any illustration, called the copyright, which is quite literally the right to withhold permission to reproduce it from anyone who has not paid an appropriate fee. The buyer of a magazine, or a book, does not acquire the right to reproduce illustrations or text from it.

There is one exception, 'clip art', which is sold with the right, sometimes circumscribed to non-commercial use or otherwise limited, to reproduce at will.

How to stay out of court—or worse

Overleaf: 16 spreads chosen at random from *Illustration* by Vicky Squires. See how her grid differs from Hugh Skinner's and mine—on the same size and shape of page. And notice how she emphasizes illustrative flow with text runarounds.

1 What is the purpose of your illustration?

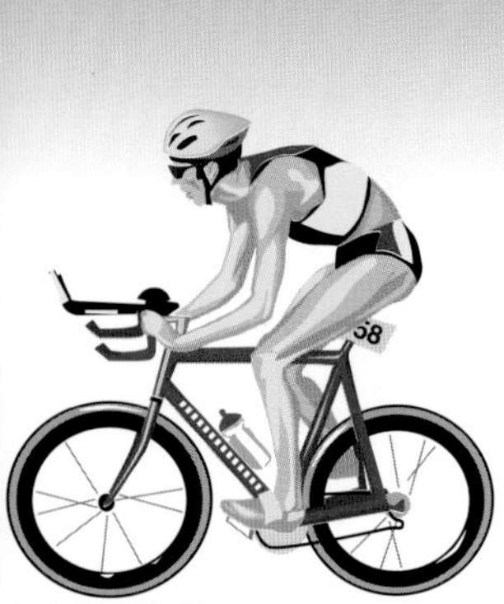

From 'Coming into Hospital'. An information booklet in nine languages for patients with little English. The illustrations add little to the understanding, but help make the publication more approachable.

Decorative or instructional?

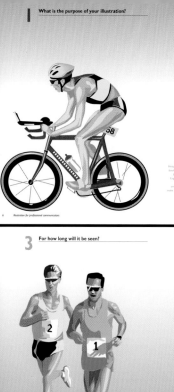

Illustrations can range in purpose from the wholly decorative to those which can stand alone and convey a message without the addition of words. The following diagram is intended to show a breakdown of the various types of illustration work – the main point being that purely decorative work is a very small proportion of the whole.

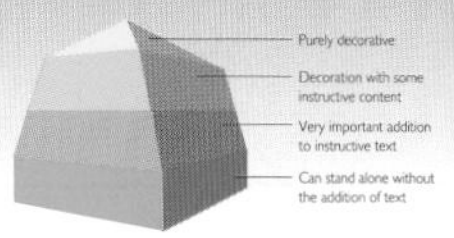

Purely decorative
Decoration with some instructive content
Very important addition to instructive text
Can stand alone without the addition of text

Purely decorative

This is the end of the illustration spectrum which offers the most artistic freedom. It's illustration for its own sake; the text can be understood perfectly well without it.

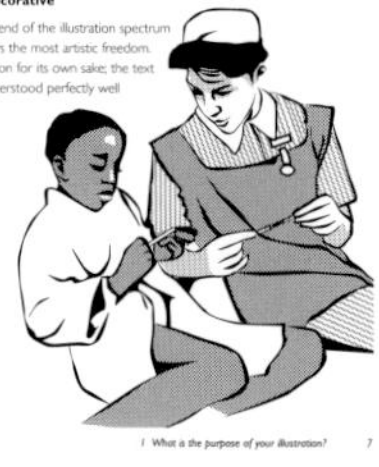

Decorative, with some instructive content

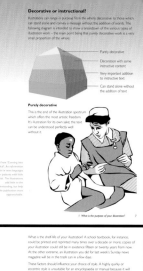

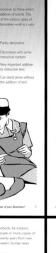

Charts and diagrams for newspapers, illustrations of products for magazines, food items for cookery books are examples of the type of image that fall into this category. 'Can you do something exciting with this chart? There are hardly any pics in this article' is usually the kind of introduction you get to this type of work. It usually involves working at great speed with very few constraints, and can be very stimulating.

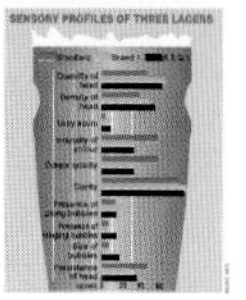

SENSORY PROFILES OF THREE LAGERS

Figures were supplied for this 'filler' diagram for Marketing Director International, Cornhill Publications.

When tackling such a job, it is best to start with a brainstorming session; quickly jot down any visual images that come to mind. Then see what you have available in the way of reference or existing images. A computer has a great advantage over traditional methods here, as you can snatch previously-generated images, modify them by changing colour, line-thickness and so on, and drop them into your new chart.

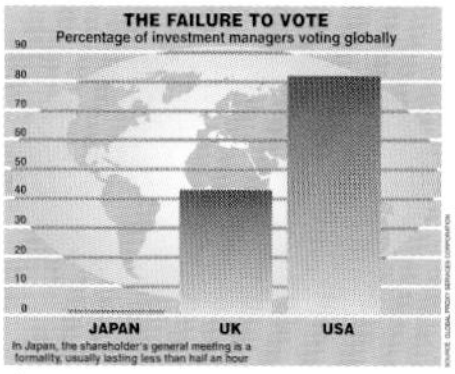

THE FAILURE TO VOTE
Percentage of investment managers voting globally
90
80
70
60
50
40
30
20
10
0
JAPAN
UK
USA
In Japan, the shareholder's general meeting is a formality, usually lasting less than half an hour

Here again, figures were supplied in the form of a bar chart. With only three bars, it had little visual interest. A world map stored on the computer from previous work made a good background, and yet the whole diagram took very little time. From Global Investment Management, Cornhill Publications.

A very important addition to an instructive text

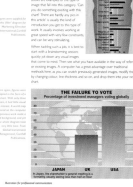

The text contains all the information required, but a picture is essentia describe a difficult action or manoeuvre. Illustration is often preferred t photography for this kind of use. Whereas a photograph would include everything in detail, an illustration need only include the details in quest other areas can be simplified, or left out entirely. There are no pedestr litter, cyclists and so on in this street as there doubtless would have be photograph of a similar scene. We don't want to distract attention fror main point of this picture, which is the action of the motor vehicles.

It's also possible to choose an odd angle of perspective. Viewed from s level, it would have been difficult to show these manoeuvres, but a bird view adds a great deal of clarity.

From The Driving Manual (HMSO/DSA).

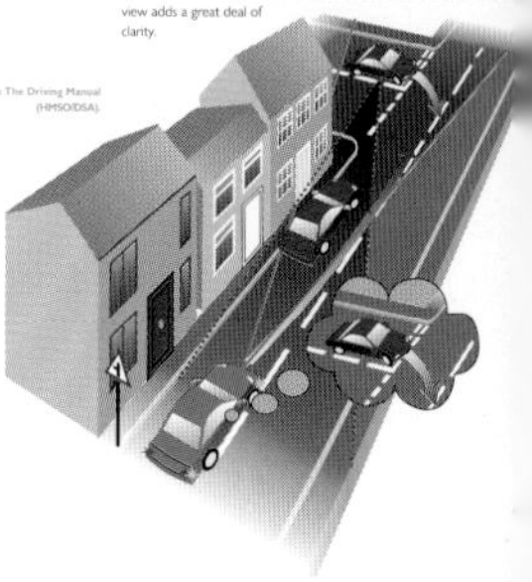

3 For how long will it be seen?

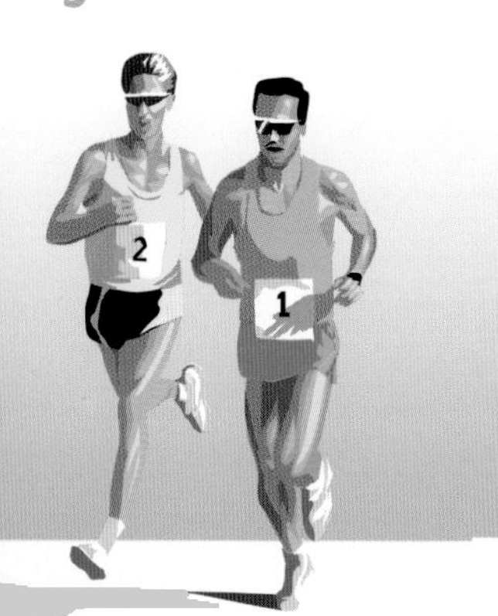

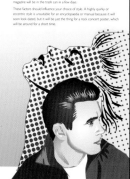

What is the shelf-life of your illustration? A school textbook, for instance, could be printed and reprinted many times over a decade or more; copies of your illustration could still be in existence fifteen or twenty years from now. At the other extreme, an illustration you did for last week's Sunday news magazine will be in the trash can in a few days.

These factors should influence your choice of style. A highly quirky or eccentric style is unsuitable for an encyclopaedia or manual because it will soon look dated, but it will be just the thing for a rock concert poster, which will be around for a short time.

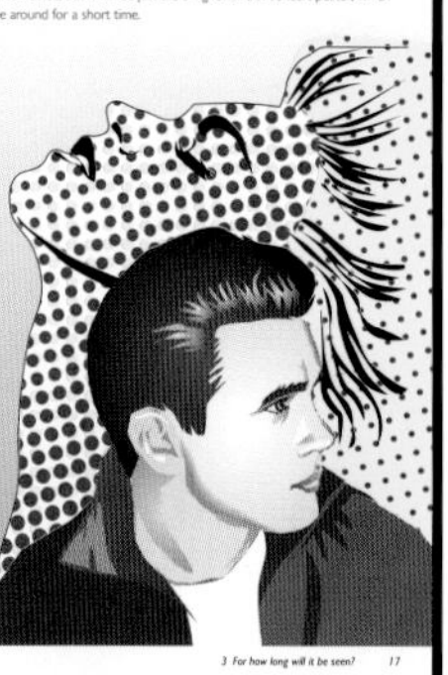

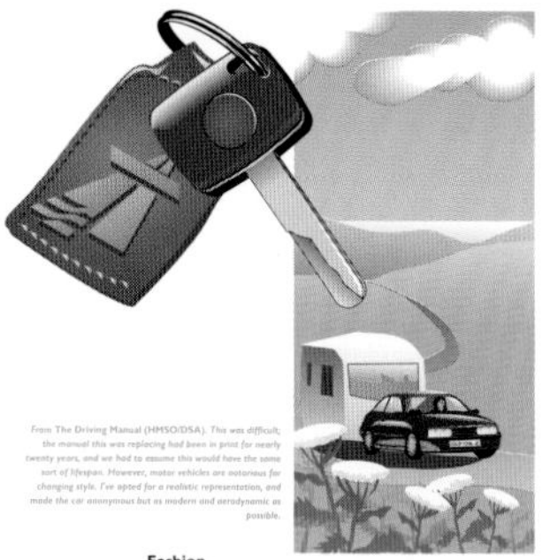

From The Driving Manual (HMSO/DSA). This was difficult; the manual this was replacing had been in print for nearly twenty years, and we had to assume this would have the same sort of lifespan. However, motor vehicles are notorious for changing style. I've opted for a realistic representation, and made the car anonymous but as modern and aerodynamic as possible.

Fashion

The main problem with fashion, be it in illustration, clothes, or music, is that it is usually followed by a rebound period when that same fashion can seem tedious and sometimes even ridiculous. A novel illustration style appears, and before long it is widely copied. The market is flooded with it, and everywhere we look we see examples – sometimes well-executed, sometimes not. Before long, boredom sets in and the style is rejected. This is unfortunate for you if it's the only style in your repertoire!

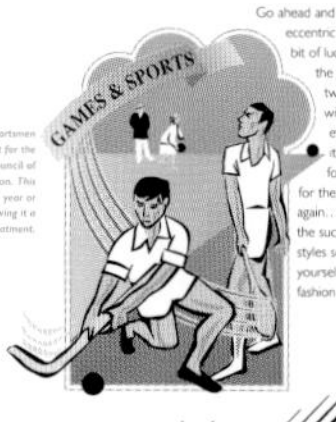

GAMES & SPORTS

These sportsmen illustrated a leaflet for the Central Council of Physical Recreation. This is reprinted every year or two, so I felt safe giving it a free and quirky treatment.

Go ahead and cultivate your highly eccentric style by all means. W bit of luck it will become 'flav the month', and for a yea two you will be inundat with work, and copied b everybody. Make the r it, but don't expect it t forever, and do brace y for the 'Oh, not that old styl again…' backlash that may fo the success. Cultivate some styles so that you don't find yourself suddenly redundant fashion moves on.

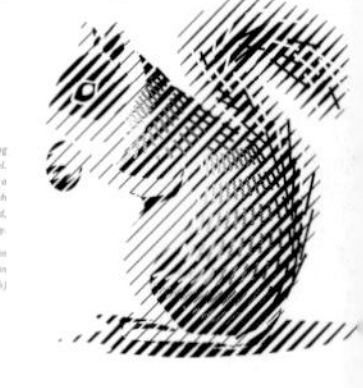

A 'woodcut' style for an advertising leaflet for Down Hall, a high class hotel. Here again, it was likely to have a lifespan of only a year or so, at which point it would probably be redesigned, and I felt able to approach it quite freely.

(This is one of a series of illustrations in the leaflet. I discuss the whole series in greater detail on pp 60-65 of this book)

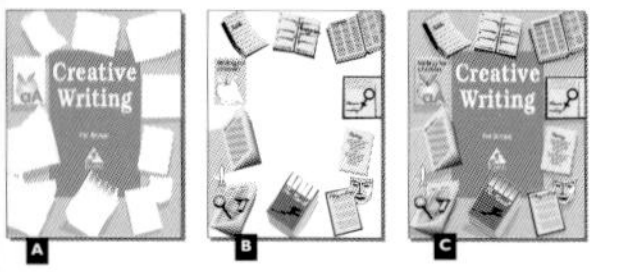

Creative Writing
A
B
C

On the two-colour book cover shown here, **A** shows what is printed by the green plate, **B** shows the black plate, and **C** the finished printed result, a composite of the two. This information was given to the printer in the form of **positive film separations**, one for the black and one for the green areas. Note the use of tints of both black and green to give an added richness to the illustrations.

Another rather more daring technique is to use two colours which can overprint each other to produce a third; yellow and blue to produce green, or yellow and red to produce orange, for example. The most commonly used printing inks are transparent and can be successfully overlaid this way. The main drawback of this technique is that you lose the definition which black always achieves. Secondly, it can be a bit of a hit-and-miss technique choosing two colours which produce an attractive, contrasting, third colour. Colour swatch books printed on transparent material are available, and it's possible to hold the two colours together and check exactly what colour you will achieve.

If you use the **process colours** (cyan, yellow, magenta and black) the colours can be gauged more accurately. These are the tried and tested shades which are used throughout the print industry to produce the full spectrum of colours in four-colour work. Charts showing the colours that can be achieved are much more readily available. Here again, don't forget to overlay tints as well as solids to get as wide a range of colours as possible.

Technical tips

Here are some examples of effects easily achieved by the computer, which were traditionally time-consuming and expensive (and in some cases, impossible!).

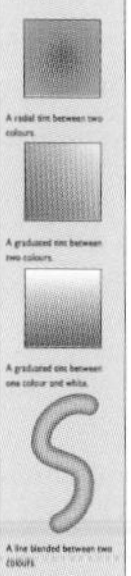

A radial tint between two colours.

A graduated tint between two colours.

A graduated tint between one colour and white.

A line blended between two colours.

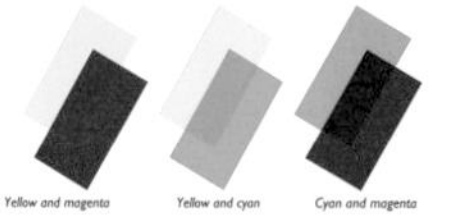

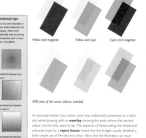

Yellow and magenta *Yellow and cyan* *Cyan and magenta*

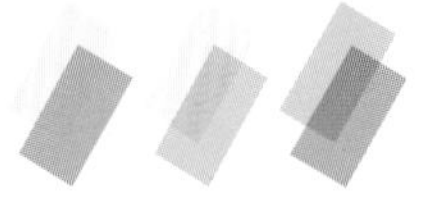

50% tints of the same colours, overlaid

As discussed earlier, two-colour work was traditionally presented as a black and white drawing with an **overlay** showing the areas where the second colour, and its tints, were to be. The expense of hand-cutting the tinted and coloured areas by a **repro house** meant that the budget usually dictated a fairly simple use of the second colour. Now that the illustrator can issue positive film separations direct to the client, the options are limitless. The computer has the capacity to produce graduated tints, subtle blends and radial tints, which would be time-consuming if tackled conventionally. This all adds to the illustrator's armoury of techniques. A richness of image can now be achieved which would have been totally impossible a decade ago.

Three-colour printing

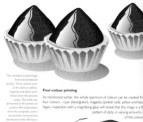

This isn't used very frequently – when one has gone to the expense of using three colours, why not run to four? However, it does crop up occasionally. Many of the points we've discussed in two-colour work apply equally to three-colour printing, i.e. clean, bright colours can be printed on top of one another to create a further one; don't forget to use tints of all the colours; if one of the colours is black, or a fairly dark tone, it will give stronger definition.

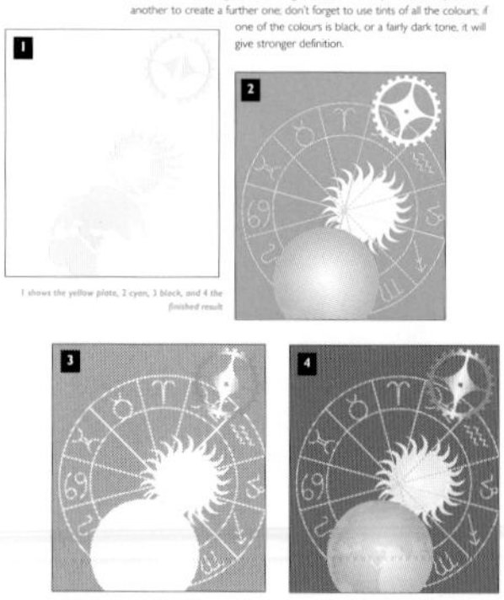

1
2
3
4

1 shows the yellow plate, 2 cyan, 3 black, and 4 the finished result

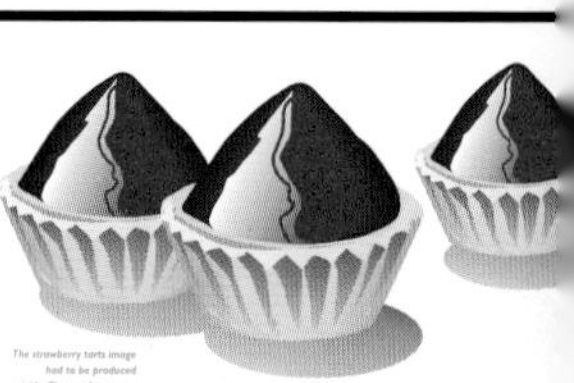

The strawberry tarts image had to be produced quickly. Three colours were to be used, so yellow, magenta and black were chosen from the process range. The work was presented to the printer as positive film separations from the computer, and it was printed, trimmed and distributed within 48 hours.

Four-colour printing

As mentioned earlier, the whole spectrum of colours can be created fro four colours – cyan (blue/green), magenta (pinkish red), yellow and blac Again, inspection with a magnifying glass will reveal that the image is a fi pattern of dots, in varying amounts o of the colour

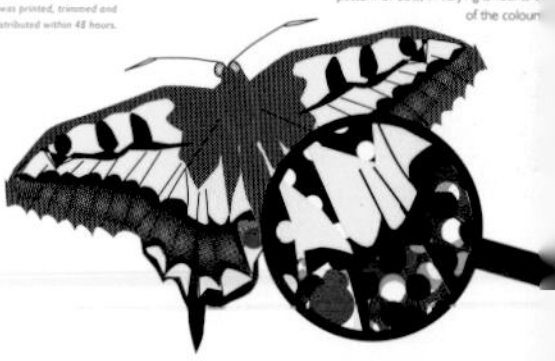

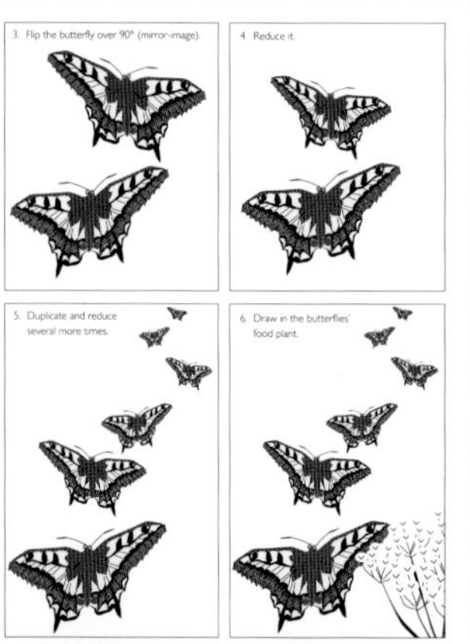

3. Flip the butterfly over 90° (mirror-image).
4. Reduce it.
5. Duplicate and reduce several more times.
6. Draw in the butterflies' food plant.

Create a few more flower heads, by duplicating your first flower, changing its size and mirror-imaging it (as you did with the butterflies). Drop in a simple background of a graduated tint of blue, and you have a whole new illustration, completed in under an hour.

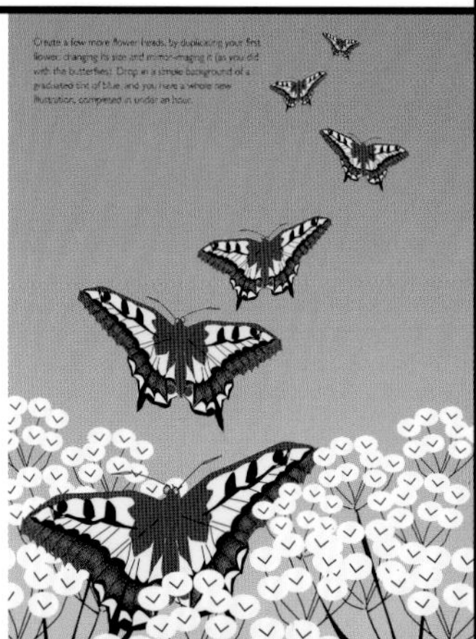

6 What are your own particular skills?

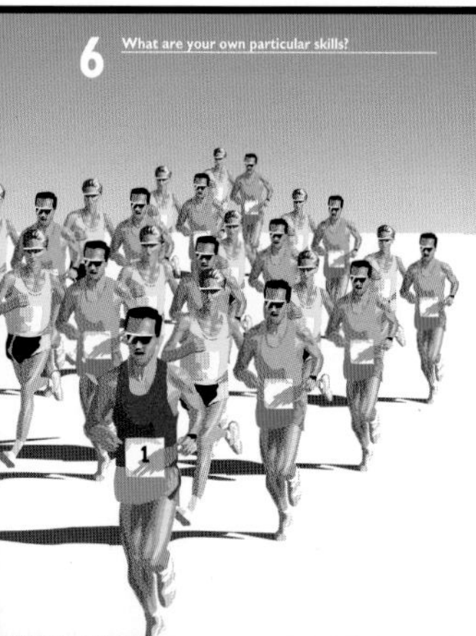

Now we come to the last and most important part of the process – YO

No illustrator is good at every subject and style. It's worth pausing for a w to analyse your own strengths and weaknesses. Why not jot down a quic in two columns? This is the beginning of mine:

Strengths	*Weaknesses*
Glass	*Hands*
Eyes	*Animals*
Skies	*Motor vehicles*

Having recognized your weaknesses, don't just use it as an excuse for tur down every project that contains them from now on! With good referen you should be able to make a professional job of anything you may encounter.

The computer is a great asset in this. I find that I enjoy drawing profiles w are facing left, but have tremendous difficulty with those facing right. (On discussion, this seems to be shared with many artists – perhaps it's a phenomenon linked to left- or right-handedness.) Now, I comfortably dra everyone facing left, and flip the image where necessary. A difficult item, l hand, need only be drawn once and can then be duplicated and transfor for further use.

Some piano-playing hands for a maths textbook – only one hand was drawn, and the others were created by duplicating the first, flipping it over and changing the colour.

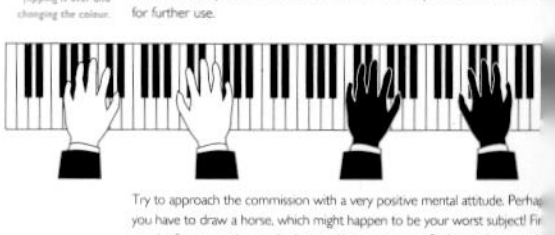

Try to approach the commission with a very positive mental attitude. Perha you have to draw a horse, which might happen to be your worst subject! Fi good reference and trace the image, then go one step further and try to ad something which you are very good at. You may be particularly skilled at cre the look of leather, for instance; add a beautifully-observed saddle or harnes

Who is it for?

Old? Young?

Relaxed? Under pressure?

Race? Gender?

Sexual stereotyping

How will it be reproduced?

Black and white illustration

Technical tips

Photocopies and laser prints

Technical tips

More than four-colour printing

How much time has been allowed?

Good reference

Screen clash

Silk screen

Special

Spot varnish

Still video camera

TIFF

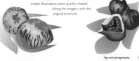

Bibliography

Drawing techniques and inspiration
Gordon, Louise. *The figure in action*. (B. T. Batsford, 1990)
Lewis, Brian. *An introduction to illustration*. (Apple Press, 1987)
Simpson, Ian (Editor). *The new guide to illustration*. (Phaidon, 1990)
White, Gwen. *Perspective*. (B. T. Batsford, 1989)

Printing Techniques
Braham, Bert. *The graphic arts studio manual*. (Collins Sons & Co Ltd, 1987)
Information Transfer. *The print book*. (National Extension College, 1985)
Laing, John (Editor). *Do-it-yourself graphic design*. (Ebury Press, 1984)
McCann, Richard. *Graphics handbook*. (Heath Education Council, 1986)

Business skills for the illustrator
Goslett, Dorothy. *The professional practice of design*. (B. T. Batsford date?)

How do you choose colour?

Experienced designers will unblushingly tell you they select colours because they like them. Don't believe it! They have become so used to applying their favourite theory or theories of colour selection that they can fly on auto-pilot when they select a set of colours —the jargon is **gamut**—for a new job. No designer ever selects colours at random. Most of us select colours because they are either adjacent to or opposite each other on Johannes Itten's useful **colour wheel**, or bear some other geometric relationship to each other across the wheel.

Above right we have the subtlety of **monochrome harmony**, so called because only one colour is chosen in each run and then diluted with white to produce a range of **tints**.

The centre group shows analogous or **related harmony**, where the colours selected are neighbours on the wheel.

At the bottom is **contrast harmony**, with the contrasts chosen from across the colour wheel. We show two contrasts but one should be enough for most designs.

W hile a design job is still in progress the designer is already specifying colour every time he chooses a colour either onscreen or by writing on his art the **cyan-magenta-yellow-black specification** for **full colour** elements (overleaf). An illustrator defines a colour with every stroke. But sometimes a colour is special, either because the designer believes the exact hue is critical to the design or because the client considers it part of his image. Then that colour requires to be precisely the same wherever in the world it is applied to the client's stationery, advertising and other publications.

This is where **spot** colours come in. Every spot colour costs one extra run through the press but the maker of the spot ink absolutely guarantees its constancy. The blue in the *Writers News* logotype is Pantone 300 and is always so specified on the company letterheads. But for the cover I didn't think an extra run worthwhile and had the blue **separated** to its constituent parts of 100C+43M+0Y+0K and printed with the rest of the full colour graphics.

Another way in which the word 'spot' is used is for one or two (but usually no more) **block colours**, often printed with black instead of full colour.

You can control critical colours by choosing 'spot' colour

W hat remains is to print your design. In theory process or four colour printing is simple. The art—illustration, photograph, handlettering, whatever—is photographed through a glass plate called a **raster** on which is drawn regularly spaced fine lines at right angles to each other. The raster turns the lines and fills of the art into **dots**. At the same time coloured filters on the camera splits the art into its cyan, magenta, yellow and black **colour components**. The raster is rotated for each colour component so that the dots will print in a **rosette** beside rather than over each other.

From the resulting **separated films** printing plates are made. Water separates the ink from the non-printing spaces on the plates, the imprint is transferred to paper, with one run through the press for each of the three colours and black, and, presto, full colour printing.

The practice is sadly different. Many of the finer details in these steps can go wrong. Your first task in a design job is always to consult the bureau and the printer and ask if they have any preferences about how you should handle and present the art.

The great imperative is to obtain the best possible art to start with. If you cannot do that, **preprocess** the art, as we did when we **posterized** (reduced the number of colours in) the cover photograph for the magazine—see page 34. You can either do this on the desktop, send the art out to specialist houses, or ask your bureau to do the work. In any case it is cheaper than later having pieces of film cut up and replaced.

Full colour printing: 'process printing'

How to quickstep through a job

On page 96 there is the usual formal index to this book. The less complete pictorial summary here is for those who prefer visual mnemonics and serves also as a rough step-by-step guide to any design job. The bold numbers are initial page references to the main entries for any subject. Turn the pages for more.

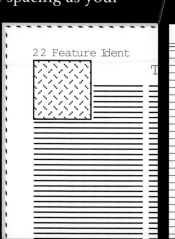

22 Feature Ident

minimum indivisible unit of space **58**. Choose a display face **60**.

Make a complete dummy **72**. Order all illustrations **79**, **87**. Lay down type and illustration specifications for control and ease of layout in other hands **62**, **86**; see **12** for what happens if you don't.

Design the special pages like the contents **70** and the cover **28**; see also section on colour **90**. Specify colour **27**, **90**.

Check proofs **91** and hand over the job to the marketing department.

We started by defining a publication as a tool in the business of communication and, at its best, as an instrument of persuasion.

We saw that David St John Thomas was satisfied with the magazines used as examples in this book. In his own words: 'Good design helped my dream come true.' His target market has also been persuaded: his magazines not only survive but grow with every issue.

So what about our other example: this book? If you're still reading, it persuades!

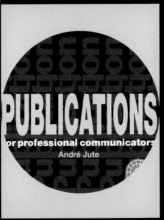

Index

—see also task order summary pp94-5